THE WRITINGS
OF SAINT FRANCIS

© Edizioni Porziuncola
Via Protomartiri Francescani, 2
06088 S. Maria degli Angeli – Assisi (PG)
www.edizioniporziuncola.it

ISBN 88-270-0060-7

Ristampa: giugno 2007

THE WRITINGS
OF SAINT FRANCIS
OF ASSISI

TRANSLATED BY IGNATIUS BRADY O.F.M.

WITH WOODCUT ILLUSTRATIONS
BY GIANLUIGI UBOLDI

EDIZIONI PORZIUNCOLA

CONTENTS

Part III: Francis Inspires the Poor Clares

Part IV: St. Francis and his Lay Followers

Part V: Francis and the Clergy

Part VI: Francis and Italy

Part VII: Francis and Ecology

THE WRITINGS OF SAINT FRANCIS

An Introduction

In The Name of the Lord

One of the most intriguing stories about Saint Francis (which in all likelihood is not pure legend) places him in the woods that once surrounded the little church of the Porziuncola[1]. Returning from prayer, he is met at the edge of the forest by his companion, Brother Masseo of Marignano, who seeks to discover how humble Francis really is. Teasingly he cries out to him: "Why after you? Why after you? Why after you?" A bit bewildered, Francis answers: "What are you trying to say? What do you mean?" "This", Masseo replies: "Why does all the world seem to be running after you and wanting to see you and hear you and obey you? You're not a very handsome man; you don't have great learning or wisdom!

---

1. Cf. The *Actus Beati Francisci et Sociorum,* ch. 10 (ed. Paul Sabatier, Paris 1902), pp. 39-40. The incident is repeated in the mediaeval Italian version known as the *Fioretti*; for an English rendition, cf. R. Brown, *The Little Flowers of St. Francis* (New York, 1958), ch. 10, pp. 62-63.

You're not of noble blood! So why is it that all the world is coming to you?"

Caught up in God, Francis eventually answers Masseo: "You want to know why after me? why? Because God did not find a greater sinner than me or one more simple and foolish, and so He chose me because He has chosen the foolish things of the world to put to shame the wise, and the base things of the world to bring to naught the noble and great and strong!".

Small wonder then that Brother Masseo was deeply moved by such an answer and was thus reassured that Saint Francis was grounded in genuine humility and was in very truth the lowly disciple of Christ. We should add that in the two following chapters of the Fioretti Francis in turn tests the humility of Fra Masseo!

Who Was Francis of Assisi?

At the end of the twelfth century one might have asked whether any good could come out of Assisi, torn as it was by factions within and rivalry without, especially against nearby Perugia. But at the end of the thirteenth century people of many nations could but wonder at the change God had worked not only in that town but throughout Europe as well and, indeed, in far-distant lands, through Saint Francis and his many holy followers.

From what we know of Assisi when the Lady Pica gave birth (about 1182) to the first of two sons, no great future could be predicted for the town or for him, later legends notwithstanding. Religion was more of a habit and tradition than of genuine conviction; political conditions were unstable, in part because of constant friction between the higher class and the ordinary citizens. Yet in the Providence of God that son, baptized John while his father, Pietro di Bernardone, was absent in France on the business of a cloth-merchant, and then dubbed Francis by the father, was eventually to be the man who would awaken and rejuvenate Assisi (and, indeed, much of Italy) and bring the people back to God.

What an unlikely choice, from our point of view! His first biographer, Friar Thomas of Celano, was to say quite bluntly that young Francis proved more of a gay blade than the son of a cloth-merchant, a hail-fellow well met, who wasted the first twenty-five years of his life in dreams of greatness. At the same time, Thomas does admit that Francis was also affable and thoughtful of others.

At twenty (late in the year 1202), he deemed himself ready for great things. He would ride, fully accoutered in the finest armor, astride the best horse Assisi could provide, to win honors for himself against the enemy, the citizens of the nearby town of Perugia. The battle (in November 1202) took place at Collestrada, along the road to Perugia. The enemy was stronger, and the Assisians who were not killed were captured (Francis among them) and ignominiously thrown into prison at Perugia.

Sick in body as well as in spirit, the would-be hero was ransomed at last, but was still weak for months to come. Yet his convalescence does not seem to have dampened his chivalrous desire to become a great knight. Indeed, once again in good health, he planned to join, with others from Assisi, the troops of Walter of Brienne, leader of the Papal forces of Innocent III in southern Italy.

At this point the Lord intervened. Details are admittedly a mite confused, since the *First Life* of Francis by Thomas of Celano lacks the precision of the *Second Life* and of the *Legend* compiled later by Saint Bonaventure. The first step in his new life was an act of generosity toward a poor but noble knight in rags and tatters (omitted in the *First Life*). Francis exchanges garments with him as Saint Martin had done in times long past for an unfortunate beggar. His reward correspondingly varies: in the *First Life* he dreams that his father's house is filled with arms, shields and lances, saddles and swords, while a voice promises that all these riches are for him and his knights. Then, in the *Second Life* the house becomes a palace in which a most beautiful bride awaits Francis: Lady Poverty, as he would learn later. The bride is hinted at, in another context, in the *First Life*, n. 7; but is completely omitted in Saint Bonaventure's *Longer Legend*, n. 3, in the same context.

Dreams, dreams! But Francis had yet one lesson to learn. Still a man of the world, he departed for southernmost Italy and the knights of the Papal army under the command of Walter of Brienne. At the end of the first day he took lodging at Spoleto, only to hear a voice in the night which asked him what he planned to do. When he explained that he wanted to go to Apuglia (on the east coast of the boot of Italy) to join the papal troops, a further question was put to him: "Who is more important, the servant or the Master?" (that is, man or Christ). When he answered: "The Master", he was told: "Why then do you seek the servant instead of the Master? Go home, for what I have shown you in the vision [of the palace] will be fulfilled in you by Me, but in a spiritual way".

When he reached Assisi, he shrugged off questions on his unwonted joy of spirit, playfully declaring that he would become a great prince. In reality, it was the beginning of his conversion. He began to pray in a cave near the town, asking the Lord of glory to direct his steps and teach him to do His will, for he was unsure of himself, so unaccustomed was he to the ways of God. Little by little he came to know what the Lord wanted of him: victory over self, abandonment of family and friends, money and worldly honor, in a life centered on God alone. If we read his *Testament* (in this volume), dictated to Brother Leo shortly before his death, we get some glimpse of the change that took place within him and the new pattern of life which he and the brothers who flocked to him began to lead, in faith, in prayer, in poverty.

A turning point in his new life was surely the visit he made to the tumble-down church of San Damiano in Assisi, which for long had been abanded by all. He knelt before the image of Christ crucified. Suddenly the lips moved and a voice said: "Francis, repair My house which, as you see, is completely in ruins". Wholly astonished at such a command, and not a little shaken, he set about to do as he was commanded. And as he did, he felt a great change within himself: his heart, his whole being, was caught up to Christ in love, and thereafter he could never think or speak of Christ Crucified without weeping. The church he thus repaired was to become, a few years later, the first home of Lady Clare and her early followers (1212), as Francis had prophesied (II Celano, n. 13). A second church, dedicated to Saint Peter, restored by Francis, seems lost in history. The third, Our Lady of the Angels, is to be found under the dome of the great Basilica of the Porziuncola. It soon became the center for Francis and the growing number of those who came to join the Lesser Brothers, the Friars Minor. It was there that Francis died at sundown on Saturday, October 3 (or according to the Umbrian way of calculating the day from sundown, in the first hours of October 4).

The intervening years had indeed been blessed by the Lord. Other men of Assisi and the neighboring towns had early been drawn to follow Francis and leave all for Christ. They were soon joined by others from all parts of Italy and, somewhat later, from almost the whole of Europe. Ere long, led by the zeal and example of Francis, they would go forth to bring new life to Christians or seek to bring the faith to unbelievers. In 1220, five would be martyred in Morocco; Francis himself and others would have gone to the East and possibly to the Holy Land; somewhere, he would meet the Sultan himself.

His real goal was martyrdom, but the Lord did not grant him that grace. He was to return to Assisi to write a new Rule of Life for the brothers, eventually approved in revised form by Pope Honorius III (1223); to celebrate the birth of Christ at what was perhaps the first Christmas crib (Greccio 1223); and to be signed with the wounds of Christ (the Stigmata) in hands and feet and side on Mount La Verna (1224).

The following year, warned by severe illnesses of his approaching death, he revealed his inner spirit of joy when in a hut at San Damiano, by now the flourishing convent of Saint Clare and her Poor Ladies, he composed the Canticle of Brother Sun, as well as another Song for the encouragement and consolation of the Sisters. Both were an expression of his desire ever to give glory to the "Most High, Omnipotent, Good Lord" in all circumstances of life.

A tiring journey (in 1225-1226) to San Fabiano and then to Siena, to consult physicians on his eyes, brought no relief. Returned to Assisi, he rested in the Palace of the Bishop for some months, and there dictated his Testament to Brother Leo. A precious document in which he recalls and celebrates the graces given him by the Lord from his conversion to his last days, it is at the same time an earnest exhortation to his Brothers to be faithful to their calling, to the Order and to the Rule, to love and venerate the Church and the Papacy, to have faith and confidence in her priests, reverence and love for the Eucharist, and total fidelity and concern for the people of God.

A few days before his death Francis was brought from the palace to his beloved Porziuncola, since he wished to die there, in the Little Portion that the Lord had given him on this earth. Some years after his death Brother Leo gave a vivid portrait of life and death of the Seraphic Saint to the

Franciscan writer and chronicler, Salimbene of Parma (d. 1288), who later wrote: "Never in the history of this whole world was there anyone other than the Blessed Francis on whom Christ imprinted the five wounds in likeness to Himself. For, as Brother Leo, his companion, who was present when his body was washed for burial, told me, Francis truly seemed like a man who had been crucified and taken down from the Cross".

From the Porziuncola that worn-out body was carried for burial to the Church of Saint George, where as a young lad he had been taught the rudiments of faith, where indeed he had learned to read and write, and where much later had begun to preach. In the same little church, on Sunday, July 16, 1228, he was to be canonized by Pope Gregory IX, who as friend and protector had known and loved Francis. Later, on May 25, 1230, his sacred remains were transferred to the Basilica which had been built in his honor, a holy place frequented ever since by all pilgrims to Assisi.

Our Edition

Essentially, this booklet presents the Writings and Dictates of Saint Francis ("Brother Leo, write!"), with a brief introduction to put each piece in proper perspective: the prayers of Francis, the Rules he wrote for his "Lesser Brothers", the Friars Minor, together with some directives for Saint Clare and her Sisters; Exhortations (or Admonitions) to his sons; others to the "Faithful", his lay-followers; and one Letter at least (in two versions) to the priests of the Lord; and his last Testament, so rich in gratitude to God for his life and mission, even as he prays that his followers be ever faithful to what they have promised the Lord.

More than once Francis apologizes because his letters, admonitions, and rules are simple in style and totally unadorned. In reality, they are more often gems of true Christian wisdom. God works indeed in mysterious ways His lessons to impart: indeed, the Writings of Saint Francis truly bear the imprint of the Holy Spirit, Who drew the whole world after Francis.

fr. Ignatius Brady O.F.M.

Grottaferrata (Roma)
15 january 1983

Part I

FRANCIS
PRAISES GOD

A PRAYER BEFORE THE CRUCIFIX

The first biographer of St. Francis, Thomas of Celano, says bluntly that for the first twenty-five years of his life Francis wasted his time on the vanities of the world. Then touched by the grace of God, he called upon the Lord to show him what he was to do (First Life, n. 2). His cry for help is expressed in this prayer, especially in its simpler form: (1°).

Another, slightly different form, in use in the English-speaking world (how widely, we cannot say) corresponds to the text as published by the Irish Franciscan historian Luke Wadding (2°).

A PRAYER BEFORE THE CRUCIFIX

1°

O most high, glorious God, enlighten the darkness of my heart and give me a right faith, a certain hope and a perfect love, understanding and knowledge, O Lord, that I may carry out Your holy and true command.

2°

O great and glorious God, and my Lord Jesus Christ, enlighten, I beseech Thee, the darkness of my mind. Give me a right faith, a certain hope, and a perfect charity. Grant that I may know Thee, Lord, in order that I may always and in all things act according to Thy most holy and perfect will. Amen.

THE CANTICLE OF BROTHER SUN

A note in the Assisi manuscript 338, folio 33, reads: "Here begin the Praises of the Creatures which the Blessed Francis made to the Praise and Honor of God while he was ill in San Damiano". The Canticle is truly the climax of a life of praise of the Creator; indeed, Thomas of Celano says that as the three youths in the fiery furnace (Daniel, 3, 17 and 23) called upon all the elements to praise and glorify the Creator of all, so Saint Francis, filled with the spirit of God, never ceased to glorify, praise and bless the Creator and Lord of all in all elements and creatures (I Cel., n. 80). Translations in English are often at fault, for this is not a song about creatures, but a joyful praise of the Lord composed by a Saint who in the midst of great suffering retained a heart full of joy in the Lord, and then at the end added the verse on Sister Death, to die with such a song on his lips and in his heart (II Cel. nn. 213-217).

THE CANTICLE OF BROTHER SUN

1 Most High, omnipotent, good Lord,
   To You praise, glory and honor and all benediction.
2 To You alone, Most High, do they belong,
   And there is no one worthy to mention You.
3 Praised be my Lord,
   by means of all Your creatures,
   and most especially by Sir Brother Sun,
   Who makes the day, and illumines us by his light:
4 For he is beautiful and radiant with great splendor;
   And is a symbol of You, God most High.
5 Praised be my Lord,
   by means of Sister Moon and all the stars:
   For in heaven You have placed them,
   clear, precious and fair.
6 Praised be my Lord, by means of Brother Wind,
   And by means of the air, the clouds,
   and the clear sky and every kind of weather,
   through which You give Your creatures nourishment.
7 Praised be my Lord, by means of Sister Water:
   For she is very useful, humble, precious and chaste.

8 Praised be my Lord, by means of Brother Fire,
  By whom You do illumine the night:
  For he is fair and gay and mighty and strong.
9 Praised be my Lord,
  by means of our sister Mother Earth,
  Which sustains us and keeps us,
  And brings forth varied fruits
  with colored flowers and leaves.
10 Praised be my Lord,
  through those who give pardon for love of You,
  And suffer infirmity and tribulation.
11 Blessed are they who endure all in peace,
  For they, O God most High,
  will be be crowned by You.
12 Praised be my Lord, through our sister Bodily Death,
  From whom no living person can escape.
13 Woe to those who die in mortal sin!
  But blessed are those found in Your most holy Will,
  For the second death will do them no harm.
14 Praise and bless my Lord,
  And thank Him, And serve Him with great humility.

PRAISES OF THE LORD GOD MOST HIGH

A Scroll given to Brother Leo, written by Saint Francis himself.

On the reverse side of the parchment, which is preserved in the Sacro Convento (San Francesco), Assisi, is found, again in the handwriting of St. Francis, the blessing for brother Leo.

PRAISES OF THE LORD GOD MOST HIGH

1 You are the holy Lord, the only God, who work
   wonders *(Pslam 76, 15)*.
2 You are strong. You are great. You are most high.
   You are the Almighty King, You, O Holy Father,
   King of heaven and earth
3 You are three and one, the Lord God of gods;
   You are good, all good, the highest good,
   Lord God, living and true.
4 You are love, charity.
   You are wisdom, You are humility,
   You are patience, You are beauty.
   You are meekness, You are security.
   You are quietude, You are joy.
   You are our hope and gladness.
   You are justice, You are temperance.
   You are all our riches to the full.
5 You are beauty, You are meekness.
   You are protector, You are our guardian and defender;
   You are strength, You are refreshment.
6 You are our hope, You are our faith,
   You are our charity; You are all our delight.
   You are our eternal life:
   The great and wondrous Lord,
   God Almighty, merciful Savior!

THE BLESSING FOR BROTHER LEO

Brother Leo himself made some annotations in red ink on the piece of parchment:

1. In the upper margin (above the Blessing) we read:

Brother Francis two years before his death kept a Lent in the place of La Verna in honor of the Blessed Virgin Mary, the Mother of God, and of Saint Michael, from the feast of the Assumption of the holy Virgin Mary until the September feast of St. Michael. After the vision and words of the Seraph and the impression of the Stigmata of Christ in his body he made these Praises written on the other side of this sheet and wrote in his own hand, giving thanks to God for the grace bestowed on him.

2. Below the text of the Blessing Leo wrote, again in red ink:

The Blessed Francis wrote with his own hand this blessing for me, brother Leo.

3. At the lower part of the parchment is a Tau with a head (that is, a T, with a skull) from the hand of Saint Francis, as Leo notes: "In like manner with his own hand he made this sign, the Thau, and the skull".

THE BLESSING
FOR BROTHER LEO

1 May the Lord bless thee and keep thee;
  May He show His face to thee and have mercy on thee.
2 May He turn His countenance to thee and give thee peace
  (Numbers 6, 24-26).
3 The Lord Bless thee, Brother Le ஂo.

THE EXPLANATION OF THE OUR FATHER

A recent list of commentaries on the Our Father by mediaeval writers (F. Stegmüller-N. Reinhardt, Repertorium Biblicum XI, pp. 191-201) contains some 330 or more entries, including the Explanation by Saint Francis as found in a codex in Brussels. It is not recognized as his; hence there is no mention of some six other manuscripts and several editions. Who acted as scribe or secretary of Saint Francis cannot be ascertained; yet he is possessed of some patristic background, inasmuch as the phrase (in n. 2): "in the angels and in the saints" is found in a ninth-century paraphrase of the Our Father.

THE EXPLANATION
OF THE OUR FATHER

1 O most holy *Pater noster*: our Creator, Redeemer, Consoler and Savior.

2 *Who art in heaven*: in the angels and in the saints; enlightening them to know [You], for You, O Lord, are light; enkindling them to love, for You, O Lord, are love; dwelling in them and filling them with happiness, because You, Lord, are the highest Good, the [eternal] Good, from Whom is every good; without Whom there is no good.

3 *Hallowed be Your name*: may our knowledge of You ever increase in clarity, that we may know what is the breadth of Your gifts, the length of Your promises, the heights of Your majesty, and the depth of Your judgments.

4 *Your Kingdom come*: that You may reign in us through grace and make us come to Your Kingdom where there is clear vision of You, perfect love of You, blessed union with You, [and] everlasting enjoyment of You.

5 *Your will be done on earth as it is in heaven*: to the end
that we may love You with [our] whole heart by always
thinking of You; with whole soul by ever desiring You;
with our whole mind by directing all our intentions to
You, by seeking Your honor in all things; and with all
our strength by spending all our powers and senses of
body and soul in the service of Your love and in nought
else; and that we may love our neighbors even as ourselves, drawing all to Your love to the best of our
power; rejoicing in the good of others as in our own
and compassionating them in their troubles and giving
no offence to anyone (cf. 2 Cor 6, 3).

6 *Give us this day our daily bread*: Your beloved Son, our
Lord Jesus Christ, that we may keep in mind and
understand and revere the love which He had for us,
and all that He taught us and did and suffered for us.

7 *And forgive us our trespasses*: out of Your ineffable
mercy, through the power of the Passion of Your beloved Son, and through the merits and intercession of
the Most Blessed Virgin and of all Your elect.

8 *As we forgive those who trespass against us*: and what
we do not fully forgive, do You, O Lord, make us
forgive in full, that we may truly love [our] enemies for
Your sake and devotedly intercede for them before You,
not rendering anyone evil for evil (cf. I Thess 5, 15), but
in You may strive to be of help to all.

9 *And lead us not into temptation*, hidden or evident, sud-
den or persistent.

10 *But deliver us from evil*, past, present, or to come.
Glory to the Father, etc.

PRAISES TO BE SAID AT EACH OF THE HOURS OF THE OFFICE

"These are the Praises which the Blessed Francis put together" from Sacred Scripture and the Liturgy, "and was wont to say before all the Hours" [of the Office]. The manuscripts would indicate that these Praises were preceded by the Paraphrase of the Our Father: "O most holy our Father: creator, redeemer... etc." which is to be found above.

1 Holy, Holy, Holy, is the Lord God Almighty,
   He who is, and who was, and who is to come (Apoc 4, 8).
   And let us praise and exalt Him
   above all for ever! (Dan 3, 85).
2 You are worthy, O Lord our God, to receive praise,
   glory and honor and blessing (Apoc 4, 11):
   and let us praise and exalt Him above all forever!
3 The Lamb that was slain is worthy to receive power,
   and divinity, and wisdom, and strength,
   and honor, and glory, and blessing (Apoc 5, 12).
   And let us praise and exalt Him above all for ever!

4 Let us bless the Father and the Son with the Holy Spirit:
And let us praise and exalt Him above all forever!

5 All you works of the Lord, bless the Lord! (Dan 3, 57).
And let us praise and exalt Him above all forever!

6 Give praise to our God, all you His servants,
And you who revere God,
the little and the great! (Apoc 19, 5)
And let us praise and exalt Him above all forever!

7 Let the heavens and the earth praise Him,
the glorious One:
And let us praise and exalt Him above all forever!

8 And [let] "every creature in heaven and on the earth,
and under the earth, and the sea, and every creature
that is in it" (Apoc 5, 13) [praise Him];
And let us praise and exalt Him above all forever!

9 Glory be to the Father and to the Son
and to the Holy Spirit:
And let us praise and exalt him above all forever!

10 As it was in the beginning, is now, and will be forever.
Amen.
And let us praise and exalt Him above all forever!

Prayer

Almighty, most holy, most high and supreme God,
All good, the highest good, wholly good,
Who alone are good:
To You we render all praise, all glory, all grace,
All honor, all blessing and everything that is good.
So be it! So be it! Amen!

AN EXHORTATION TO PRAISE GOD

Franciscan chronicles (of Marianus of Florence and the Annals of Luke Wadding) speak of a wooden antipendium (or front) attached to an altar in the ancient Franciscan hermitage at Cesi di Terni (midway between Rome and Assisi) on which Saint Francis himself wrote verses of Scripture calling on creatures to praise their Creator. Though the original piece has disappeared, the texts Saint Francis wrote have been found in a manuscript in Naples as copied by a fifteenth-century witness from the original antipendium which by then was attached to the wall of the chapel:

AN EXHORTATION
TO PRAISE GOD

1   Fear the Lord and give Him honor (Apoc 14, 7).
2   The Lord is worthy to receive
    praise and honor (Apoc 4, 11).
3   All you who fear the Lord, praise Him (Ps 21, 24).
4   Hail Mary, full of grace,
    the Lord is with you (Lk 1, 28).
5   Praise Him,
    heaven and earth (Ps 68, 35, Roman Psalter).
6   Praise the Lord, all ye rivers (Dan 3, 78).
7   All you children of God, bless the Lord (Dan 3, 82).
8   This is the day the Lord has made:
    let us be glad and rejoice therein (Ps 117, 24).
    Response: Alleluja, Alleluja, Alleluja,
    O King of Israel (Jo 12, 13).
9   Let everything that has breath
    praise the Lord (Ps 150, 6).
10   Praise the Lord, for He is good (Ps 146, 1).
    All you who read this, bless the Lord.
11   All creatures bless the Lord (cf Ps 102, 22).
12   All you birds of the air, bless the Lord (Dan 3, 80).
13   All you children, praise the Lord (cf Ps 112, 1).
14   Young men and maidens, praise the Lord (Ps 148, 12).
15   Worthy is the Lamb that was slain
    to receive praise, glory and honor (cf. Apoc 5, 12).
16   Blessed be the Holy Trinity and undivided Unity.
17   Saint Michael the Archangel, defend us in battle.

THE SALUTATION TO OUR LADY

Thomas of Celano, the early biographer, says of Francis that, loving the Mother of Jesus with a love beyond all telling because she made the Lord of majesty our Brother, he composed special Praises in her honor (The Second Life, n. 198).

THE SALUTATION TO OUR LADY

1 Hail, O Lady, Holy Queen, God's Holy Mother Mary!
You have been made the Virgin Church
And chosen by the most Holy Father in heaven.
2 You has He consecrated with His most holy beloved Son
and the Holy Spirit the Paraclete.
3 In You there has been, and is,
all fullness of Grace, and all that is good.
4 Hail His Palace! Hail His Tabernacle!
Hail His Dwelling Place!
5 Hail His Garment![1] Hail His Handmaid!
Hail His Mother!
6 And (hail) all you holy Virtues [in her] which by the
grace and enlightenment of the Holy Spirit
are poured forth into the hearts of the faithful,
that from faithless souls
You [virtues] may make them faithful to God!

---

[1] If "Garment" may seem a strange metaphor, we note that two centuries before Saint Francis this analogy together with Palace, Tabernacle, and Dwelling Place, was used by St. Peter Damian (d. 1072)!

SALUTATION OF THE VIRTUES

Thomas of Celano vouches for the authenticity of this delightful song of praise to the virtues, since he cites the opening verse in his Second Life *of Saint Francis, n. 189, as he portrays the true simplicity of Saint Francis and its meaning for all who follow him. Two manuscripts link the virtues here praised with Our Lady:* "On the virtues which adorned the Holy Virgin and should be in every holy soul". *When Saint Francis composed this Praise cannot be determined.*

SALUTATION
OF THE VIRTUES

1   Hail, Queen Wisdom! May the Lord preserve you
    with your sister Holy pure Simplicity!
2   O Lady Holy Poverty, may the Lord save you
    with your sister Holy Humility!
3   O Lady Holy Charity, may the Lord save you
    with your sister Holy Obedience!
4   O all you most holy Virtues, may the Lord save you all,
    from Whom you come and proceed.
5   There is truly no man in the whole world
    who can possess one of you unless he first die [to self].
6   He who has one and does not offend the others,
    possesses all;
7   And he who offends one,
    possesses none and offends all (Cf. Jas 2, 10).
8   And each of them puts to rout vices and sins.
9   Holy Wisdom confounds Satan and all his wicked ways.
10 Pure holy Simplicity confounds all the wisdom
    of this world and the wisdom of the flesh.
11 Holy Poverty confounds cupidity and avarice
    and the cares of this world.
12 Holy Humility confounds pride
    and all the people who are in this world
    and in like manner all things that are in the world.
13 Holy Charity confounds all temptations that come from
    the devil or from the flesh, and all human fears
    [cf. I John 4, 18: Love has no room for fear].
14 Holy Obedience puts to rout all self-centered and carnal
    desires and 15 keeps the body subject to the obedience
    of the inner man and to obedience to one's brother, 16
    and thus a man is subject and submissive to all men
    who are in the world; 17 and not only to humans, but
    also to all beasts and wild animals, 18 so that they may
    do with him whatsoever they will, insofar as it may have
    been granted them from above by the Lord.

THE OFFICE OF THE PASSION

The introductory rubric to this Office tells us: "Here begin the Psalms which our most blessed Father Francis put together to venerate and recall to mind and to praise the Passion of the Lord. They are to be said along with the day hours [of the Office] and at the one at night [Compline]. And they begin at Compline of Good Friday [we would say, of Holy Thursday; but in the Middle Ages the new day began at sundown] because it was on that night that Our Lord Jesus Christ was betrayed and taken captive. And note that the Blessed Francis was wont to say this office thus: First he would say the prayer which the Lord and Master taught us: "Our Father, *most holy One", and so on [found elsewhere in this book], together with the* Praises *which begin:* "Holy, Holy, Holy...". *When he had finished the Lauds and its prayer [*"Almighty, Most High..."*], he would begin this antiphon, namely* "Holy Virgin Mary". *He then said the Psalms of Mary most holy; then he said other psalms which he had chosen ([verses he had put together from various psalms]; and at the end of all the psalms he would say the Psalms of the Passion [the Office here]. After each psalm [of hour] he said the antiphon* Holy Virgin Mary. *The end of this antiphon was also the end of the Office".*

However, to present the Office as found in the manuscripts, in rather shortened form and with obscure directives on its use, would but confuse anyone who might wish to pray the Office with Saint Francis. We have taken the liberty therefore to arrange the text for easier use. The Psalm-text is a combination of the old (Douay) version, close to the Latin of the Vulgate, and the New American Bible. At times the Jerusalem Bible has been consulted.

THE OFFICE
OF THE PASSION

1. IN ADVENT

Here begin the psalms which our most blessed Father Francis arranged to be said... from the Advent of the Lord until the vigil of Christmas and no further. [We have put the Hour of Vespers here, according to modern usage; this is followed by Night Prayer (Compline); and then the Day Hours of Advent, Prime, Tierce, Sext and Nones.]

At Vespers [or Evening Prayer]

The Antiphon is intoned only: *Holy Virgin Mary*.

1 All you peoples, clap your hands: * shout to God with cries of gladness!

2 For the Lord, the Most High, the awesome, * is the Great King over all the earth.

3 Because the Most Holy Father of Heaven, our King before all ages, * sent His Beloved Son from on high, and has wrought salvation in the midst of the earth.

4 Let the heavens be glad and the earth rejoice; let the sea and all that fills it be moved, * let the plains be joyful and all things that are in them.

5 Sing to the Lord a new song, * sing to the Lord, all you lands!

6 For great is the Lord and highly to be praised: * awesome is He, beyond all gods.

7 Give to the Lord, you families of nations; give to the Lord glory and honor: * give to the Lord the glory due His Name!

8 Offer up your very selves and carry His holy Cross *
and follow to the very end His most holy commandments.

9 Glory to the Father, etc.

Then follows the Antiphon [which was intoned above]:

1 Holy Virgin Mary, there is none like you born in the
world among women, 2 daughter and handmaid of the
most high King, the Father in heaven! Mother of our
most holy Lord Jesus Christ! Spouse of the Holy Spirit!
3 Pray for us, with Saint Michael the Archangel and all
the Powers of heaven and all the Saints, to Your most
holy beloved Son, our Lord and Master. 4 Glory to the
Father and to the Son and to the Holy Spirit. 5 As it
was in the beginning, is now, and will be forever.
Amen.

[Note, says the unknown scribe, that this Antiphon is said at
all the Hours, and takes the place of (other) antiphons,
chapter-verse, hymn, versicle and (concluding) prayer, both at
Matins and likewise at all the other Hours...]

At Night Prayer

Introductory Antiphon: *Holy Virgin Mary.*

1 How long, O Lord? Will You utterly forget Me? * How
long will You hide Your face from Me?

2 How long shall I harbor grief in My soul, * sorrow in
My heart day after day?

3 How long will My enemy triumph over me? * Look and
answer Me, O Lord My God!

4 Give light to My eyes that I may never sleep in death, *
lest My enemy say: I have overcome Him!

5 Those who trouble Me will rejoice in My downfall, * yet
I have trusted in Your mercy.

6 My heart shall rejoice in Your saving help; I shall sing
to the Lord who gives Me good things, * and I shall
praise the name of the Lord the most High [Ps. 12 (13),
1-6].

7 Glory to the Father and to the Son and to the Holy

Spirit. * As it was in the beginning, is now and will be forever. Amen.

Then follows, as at Vespers, the Marian Antiphon intoned above: *Holy Virgin Mary*. As concluding prayer to this Office [at the end of Night Prayer] the Blessed Francis always said:

Let us bless the Lord God living and true! Let us always render Him praise, glory, honor, blessing, and all good things!! Amen. Amen. So be it! So be it!

At Morning Prayer [Matins]

A Psalm [composed by St. Francis]
Antiphon intoned: *Holy Virgin Mary!*
1 I shall give You thanks, O Lord, most Holy Father, King of heaven and earth, * because You have consoled Me (cf. Is 12, 1).
2 You are God My Savior: * I will be full of confidence and without fear! (Is 12, 2).
3 My strength and My song is the Lord, * and He has become My salvation (ibid.).
4 Your right hand, O Lord, is magnificent in power, Your right hand, O Lord, has shattered the enemy, * and in the greatness of Your glory You have overthrown My adversaries (Exod 15, 6-7).
5 Let the poor see and be glad: * Seek the Lord, and your soul shall live (Ps 68, 33).
6 Let the heavens and the earth praise Him, * the sea and every thing that moves therein (Ps 68, 35).
7 For God will save Sion, * and the cities of Judah shall be rebuilt (Ps 68, 36).
8 And they shall dwell in the land, * and acquire it by inheritance (ibid.).
9 And the descendents of His servants shall possess it; * and they who love His name shall dwell therein.

The full antiphon:Holy Virgin Mary is said here.

At the Hour of Prime

A Psalm of St. Francis based on Ps. 56 (57)

Antiphon: *Holy Virgin Mary.*

1 Have mercy on Me, O God, have mercy on Me: * for My soul trusts in You.
2 And in the shadow of Your wings I will hope, * until iniquity pass away.
3 I will call to My most holy Father, the Most High, * to the Lord who has done good to Me.
4 He has sent from heaven and freed Me: * He has made those a reproach who trampled on Me.
5 God has sent His mercy and His faithfulness: * He has snatched My soul from My mighty enemies and from those who hate Me, for they were too powerful for Me.
6 They have prepared a snare for My feet, * and have bowed down My soul.
7 They have dug a pit before My face, * and they have fallen into it.
8 My heart is steadfast, O God! My heart is steadfast! * I will sing and chant a psalm [of praise].
9 Awake, My glory [= soul]; awake lyre and harp! * I will awake the dawn.
10 I will give praise to You among the peoples, O Lord! * I will chant Your praises among the nations!
11 For Your mercy towers to the heavens, * and Your faithfulness to the skies.
12 Be exalted above the heavens, O God, * and Your glory be above all the earth.
    The Marian Antiphon is added.

[Note that this psalm is always said at Prime] (= *a scribe's note or rubric found in some manuscripts*).

At the Hour of Tierce

Antiphon intoned: *Holy Virgin Mary*

1 Shout joyfully to the Lord, all the earth! Sing to the glory of His Name! * Proclaim His glorious praise.

2 Say to God: How awesome are Your works, O Lord! *
  Because of Your mighty power Your enemies will praise
  You unwillingly.

3 Let all the earth worship You and sing praise to You, *
  let it sing a psalm to Your Name.

4 Come, listen, and I will declare, all you who fear God,
  * what great things He has done for My soul.

5 I cried to Him with My mouth, * and I exulted with the
  tip of My tongue.

6 And He heard My voice from His holy temple, * and
  My cry reached His presence.

7 Bless our Lord, you peoples, * and make the voice of
  His praise be heard.

8 In Him shall all the tribes of the earth be blessed, * All
  nations shall glorify Him!

9 Blessed be the Lord, the God of Israel, * Who alone
  does wondrous deeds!

10 And blessed be the name of His majesty forever, * and
  the whole earth shall be filled with His majesty: Amen,
  So be it!

Here follows the Antiphon in full: *Holy Virgin Mary.*

At the Hour of Sext

Antiphon intoned: Holy Virgin Mary.

1 May the Lord hear you in the day of tribulation. * May
  the Name of the God of Jacob protect you.

2 May He send you help from His holy place, * and from
  Zion may He defend you.

3 May He remember all your sacrifices, * and may your
  burnt offerings please Him.

4 May He grant you what is in your heart * and confirm
  your every plan.

5 We shall rejoice in your victory, * and in the Name of
  the Lord our God we shall be elated.

6 May the Lord fulfill all you ask of Him! Now I know

that the Lord has sent Jesus Christ His Son * and that
He shall judge the peoples in justice.

7 And the Lord has become the refuge of the poor, a
   helper in times of distress. * And let them hope in You
   who have known Your name.

8 Blessed be the Lord my God, for He has become My
   support and My refuge * in the day of My trouble.

9 My Helper, I shall sing to You, because You are God,
   My defence, * My God, My mercy.

The full antiphon of Our Lady is recited here.

At the Ninth Hour (Nones)

Antiphon intoned: *Holy Virgin Mary.*

1 In You, O Lord, I have hoped; let Me never be put to
   shame. * In Your justice rescue Me and deliver Me.

2 Incline Your ear to me, * and save Me.

3 Be unto Me a God, a protector, * a stronghold to give
   Me safety.

4 For You are My hope, O Lord, * My trust, O Lord,
   from My youth.

5 On You have I depended since birth; from My mother's
   womb You are My Protector, * and of You shall I continually sing.

6 Let My mouth be filled with praise, that I may sing
   Your glory, * and all the day long Your greatness.

7 Hear Me, O Lord, for Your mercy is kind; * look upon
   Me according to the bounty of Your kindness.

8 And turn not Your face away from Your servant! *
   Because I am in trouble, hear Me quickly!

9 Blessed be the Lord My God, for He has become My
   support and My refuge * in the day of My distress.

10 O My Helper, I will sing Your praise, for God is My
   support! * My God, My mercy!

The Antiphon in full concludes the Hour.

2. CHRISTMASTIDE

From Vespers on Christmas Eve to the Octave of Epiphany [= the Baptism of the Lord], according to the directive of St. Francis, the following psalm is said at all the Hours. It should be prefaced by the "Praises to be said at each Hour of the Office", namely the *Holy, Holy, Holy*. Then the Antiphon: *Holy Virgin Mary* is intoned and the psalm follows. And let it be said with great devotion! [Thus the rubric!].

Antiphon: Holy Virgin Mary.

The Psalm

1 Sing joyfully to God our Strength! * Shout to the Lord God living and true with cries of gladness!

2 For the Lord, the most High, the Awesome, * is the Great King over all the earth.

3 Because the Most Holy Father of heaven, our King before all ages, sent His beloved Son from on high; * and He was born of the Blessed Virgin Holy Mary.

4 He cried out to Me: You are My Father! * and I will make Him the Firstborn, high above the kings of the earth.

5 On that day the Lord bestowed His mercy, * and at night [I have] His song.

6 This is the day the Lord has made: * let us be glad and rejoice therein.

7 For the most holy beloved Child is given to us, and was born for us on the way and was laid in a manger, * because there was no room in the inn.

8 Glory to the Lord God in the highest, * and on earth peace to men of good will.

9 Let the heavens be glad and the earth rejoice; let the sea and all that fills it resound; * let the plains be joyful and all that is in them.

10 Sing to the Lord a new song, * sing to the Lord, all the earth!
11 For great is the Lord and highly to be praised, * awesome is He, beyond all gods.
12 Give to the Lord, you families of nations, give to the Lord glory and honor; * give to the Lord the honor due His name.
13 Offer up your bodies and carry His Cross, * and observe His most holy commandments to the very end.
14 Let us bless the Lord God living and true; let us always render to Him praise, glory, honor, blessing, and all good things. Amen, Amen, Fiat, Fiat [= So be it!].

HOLY VIRGIN MARY, there is none like you born in the world among women, 2 daughter and handmaid of the most high King, the Father in heaven! Mother of our most holy Lord Jesus Christ! Spouse of the Holy Spirit! 3 Pray for us, with Saint Michael the Archangel and all the Powers of heaven and all the Saints, to Your most holy beloved Son, Our Lord and Master. 4 Glory to the Father and to the Son and to the Holy Spirit. 5 As it was in the beginning, is now, and will be forever. Amen.

3. SUNDAYS OF THE YEAR

For Sundays of the Year (*after Epiphany to Palm Sunday inclusive*); for Holy Thursday; and from the Octave of Pentecost (*now Holy Trinity*) to the Last Sunday before Advent; and on the principal Feasts which occur in such parts of the liturgical year.

At Morning Prayer [Matins]

Antiphon intoned: Holy Virgin Mary!

1   Sing a new song unto the Lord, * for He has done wondrous deeds.
2   His right hand and His holy arm * has sacrificed His beloved Son.
3   The Lord has made His salvation known: * in the sight of the nations He has revealed His justice.
4   On that day the Lord bestowed His mercy: * and at night [I have] His song.
5   This is the day the Lord has made: * let us be glad and rejoice in it.
6   Blessed is He who comes in the name of the Lord: * the Lord is God, and He has shone upon us.
7   Let the heavens be glad and the earth rejoice, let the sea and all that fills it resound: * let the plains be joyful and all that is in them.
8   Give to the Lord, you families of nations, * give to the Lord glory and praise: * give to the Lord the glory due His name!
9   Holy Virgin Mary, etc.

At the Hour of Prime

Antiphon intoned: Holy Virgin Mary!

1   Have mercy on Me, O God, have mercy on Me: * for My soul trusts in You.

2 And in the shadow of Your wings I will hope, until iniquity pass away.

3 I will call to My most holy Father, the Most High, * to the Lord who has done good to Me.

4 He has sent from heaven and freed Me: * He has made those a reproach who trampled on Me.

5 God has sent His mercy and faithfulness: * He has snatched My soul from My mighty enemies and from those who hated Me, for they were too powerful for Me.

6 They have prepared a snare for My feet, * and have bowed down My soul.

7 They have dug a pit before My face, * and they have fallen into it.

8 My heart is steadfast, O God! My heart is steadfast! * I will sing and chant a psalm [of praise].

9 Awake, My glory [= My soul]; awake lyre and harp! * I will awake the dawn.

10 I will give praise to You among the peoples, O Lord! * I will chant Your praise among the nations!

11 For Your mercy towers to the heavens, * and Your faithfulness to the skies.

12 Be exalted above the heavens, O God, * and Your glory be above all the earth.

13 Holy Virgin Mary, etc.

At the Hour of Tierce

Antiphon intoned: Holy Virgin Mary!

1 Shout joyfully to the Lord, all the earth! Sing to the glory of His Name! * Proclaim His glorious praise!

2 Say to God: How awesome are Your works, O Lord. * Because of Your mighty strength Your enemies will praise You unwillingly.

3 Let all the earth worship You and sing praise to You, * let it sing a psalm to Your Name.

4 Come, listen, and I will declare, all you who fear God, * what great things He has done for My soul.

5 I cried to Him in words, * and praise was on the tip of My tongue.

6 And from His holy temple he heard My voice, * and My cry reached His presence.

7 Bless our Lord, you peoples, * and make the voice of His praise be heard.

8 And in Him shall all the tribes of the earth be blessed. * All nations shall glorify Him.

9 Blessed be the Lord, the God of Israel, * Who alone does wondrous deeds.

10 And blessed be the Name of His majesty forever, * and the whole earth shall be filled with His majesty: Amen! So be it!.

11 Holy Virgin Mary, in full.

At the Hour of Sext

The Antiphon: Holy Virgin Mary!

1 May the Lord hear you in the day of tribulation. * May the Name of the God of Jacob protect You.

2 May He send you help from His holy place, * and from Zion may He defend You.

3 May He remember all Your sacrifices, * and may your burnt offerings please Him.

4 May He grant you what is in your heart, * and confirm your every plan.

5 We shall rejoice in your victory, * and in the Name of the Lord our God we shall be elated.

6 May the Lord fulfill all you ask of Him! Now I know that the Lord has sent Jesus Christ His Son * and that He shall judge the peoples in justice.

7 And the Lord has become the refuge of the poor, a helper in times of distress. * And let them hope in You who have known Your name.

8 Blessed be the Lord My God, for He has become My support and My refuge * in the day of My trouble.

9 My Helper, I shall sing to You, because You are God My defence. * My God, My mercy!

10 Holy Virgin Mary, in full.

At Nones (the Ninth Hour)

The Antiphon: Holy Virgin Mary!

1 In You, O Lord, I have hoped; let Me never be put to shame. * In Your justice rescue Me and deliver Me.

2 Incline Your ear to Me, * and save Me.

3 Be unto Me a God, a protector, * a stronghold to give Me safety.

4 For You are My hope, O Lord, * My trust, O Lord, from My youth.

5 On You I depend from birth; from My mother's womb You are My Protector, * and of You shall I continually sing.

6 Let My mouth be filled with praise, that I may sing Your glory, * and all the day long Your greatness.

7 Hear Me, O Lord, for Your mercy is kind; * look upon Me according to the bounty of Your kindness.

8 And turn not Your face away from Your Servant! * Because I am in trouble, hear Me quickly!

9 Blessed be the Lord My God, for He has become My support and My refuge * in the day of My distress.

10 O My Helper, I will sing Your praise, for God is My support! * My God, My mercy!

11 Holy Virgin Mary, in full.

At Evening Prayer

The Antiphon: Holy Virgin Mary.

1 All you people, clap your hands: * shout to God with cries of gladnes!

2 For the Lord, the Most High, the awesome, * is the great King over all the earth.

3 Because the Most Holy Father of heaven, our King before all ages, * sent His beloved Son from on high, and has wrought salvation in the midst of the earth.

4 Let the heavens be glad and the earth rejoice: let the sea and all that fills it be moved; * let the plains be joyful and all things that are in them.

5 Sing to the Lord a new song; * Sing to the Lord, all you lands!

6 For great is the Lord and highly to be praised: * awesome is He, beyond all gods.

7 Give to the Lord, you families of nations; give to the Lord glory and honor: * give to the Lord the glory due His Name.

8 Offer up your bodies and carry His holy Cross * and follow to the very end His most holy precepts.

9 Let all the earth tremble before Him. * Say among the nations that the Lord has reigned from the Cross.

[On the feast of the Ascension we are to add:]

10 And He ascended into heaven and is seated at the right hand of the most holy Father in heaven: Be exalted above the heavens, O God; * above all the earth be Your glory!

11 And we know that He is coming, * for He will come to judge justice.

* After 9 or 11: the antiphon Holy Virgin Mary, in full.

4. OFFICE OF THE PASSION FOR ORDINARY WEEKDAYS

For Weekdays from the Baptism of the Lord to Holy Saturday (except Holy Thursday, found in n. 3); and from Trinity Sunday to the Saturday before Advent.

At Morning Prayer (Matins)

Antiphon intoned: Holy Virgin Mary!

1　O Lord, the God of My salvation, * by day I cry out, and in the night I clamor in Your presence.

2　Let My prayer come before You: * incline Your ear to My call for help.

3　Attend to My soul and deliver it: * because of My enemies snatch Me away.

4　For it was You who drew Me out of the womb: My security at the breasts of My mother; * to You was I committed from the womb.

5　From My mother's womb You are My God: * O be not far from Me.

6　You know My reproach and My confusion, * and My ignominy.

7　In Your sight are all those who afflict Me; * My Heart has expected [such] reproach and misery.

8　And I looked for one who would grieve with Me, and there was no one! * and for one who would comfort Me, and I found none.

9　O God, the wicked have risen against Me * and the company of the powerful seek My life, nor do they set You before their eyes.

10　I am numbered with those who go down into the pit: * I have become as a man without help, free among the dead.

11　You are My most Holy Father, * My King and My God.

12　Make haste to help Me, * O Lord, the God of My salvation.

Antiphon: Holy Virgin Mary, there is none like you born in the world among women, 2 daughter and handmaid of the most high King, the Father in heaven! Mother of our most holy Lord Jesus Christ! Spouse of the Holy Spirit! 3 Pray for us, with Saint Michael the Archangel and all the Powers of heaven and all the Saints, to Your most holy beloved Son, Our Lord and Master. 4 Glory to the Father... 4 As it was in the beginning...

The Hour of Prime

Antiphon: Holy Virgin Mary!

1   Have mercy on Me, O God, have mercy on Me: * for My soul trusts in You.
2   And in the shadow of Your wings I will hope, * until iniquity pass away.
3   I will call to My most holy Father, the Most High, * to the Lord who has done good to Me.
4   He has sent from heaven and freed Me: * He has made those a reproach who trampled on Me.
5   God has sent His mercy and His faithfulness: * He has snatched My soul from My mighty enemies and from those who hated Me, for they were too powerful for Me.
6   They have prepared a snare for My feet, * and have bowed down My soul.
7   They have dug a pit before My face, * and have fallen into it.
8   My heart is steadfast, O God! My heart is steadfast! * I will sing and chant a psalm [of praise].
9   Awake my glory [= soul]! Awake lyre and harp! * I will awake the dawn!
10 I will give praise to You among the peoples, O Lord! * I will chant Your praise among the nations!
11 For Your mercy towers to the heavens, * and Your faithfulness to the skies.

12 Be exalted above the heavens, O God, * and Your glory
be above all the earth.

The Antiphon: *Holy Virgin Mary*   is said in full as above.

The Hour of Tierce

Antiphon: Holy Virgin Mary!

1 Have pity on Me, O God, for men trample on Me; * all
day long they press their attack against Me.
2 My enemies have trampled on Me all the day, * for they
are many who make war against Me.
3 All My enemies have devised evil against Me, * and imagine the worst against Me.
4-5 Those who keep watch against My life have taken
counsel together, * they have gone forth and whispered
against Me.
6 All who see Me scoff at Me; * they mock Me with
parted lips and wag their heads.
7 I am a worm, and not a man, * the scorn of men and
the outcast of the people.
8 For all My enemies I am an object of reproach, a
laughing-stock to My neighbors, and a dread to those
who know Me.
9 Holy Father, let not Your help be far from Me, * (but
rather) look to My defence.
10 Make haste to help Me, * O Lord God of My salvation!

The Antiphon: *Holy Virgin Mary* in full.

The Hour of Sext

The Antiphon: Holy Virgin Mary!

1 With a loud voice I cried to the Lord; * with a loud
voice I besought the Lord.
2 My complaint I pour out before Him; * before Him I
lay bare My distress.

3 When My spirit was faint within Me, * You have known My paths.

4 In the way on which I was walking * the proud ones hid a snare for Me.

5 I looked to the right to see, * and there was no one who would pay Me heed.

6 I had lost all means of escape, * and there was no one who cared for My life.

7 Since for Your sake I have borne insult, * shame has covered My face!

8 I have become an outcast to My brothers, * and a stranger to the sons of My mother.

9 Holy Father, zeal for Your house consumes Me, * and the insults of those who blaspheme You fall on Me.

10 And they rejoiced against Me and gathered together, * heaping blows upon Me when I did not expect them.

11 Those outnumber the hairs of My head * who hate Me without cause.

12 They have grown strong, My enemies who hate Me without cause: * must I restore what I did not steal?

13 Unjust witnesses have risen up * and asked Me things they did not know.

14 They repaid Me evil for good and harassed Me * because I pursued goodness.

15 You are My most holy Father, * My King and My God!

16 Make haste to help Me, * O Lord, the God of My salvation!

The Antiphon: *Holy Virgin Mary!* in full.

The Hour of Nones

The Antiphon: Holy Virgin Mary!

1 O all you that pass by the way, * attend and see if there is any sorrow like My sorrow.

2 For many dogs have surrounded Me, * a pack of evildoers has closed in upon Me.

3   They have looked on and gloated over Me. * They have divided My garments among them, and for My vesture they cast lots.

4   They have pierced My hands and My feet, * and have counted all My bones.

5   They have opened their mouths against Me, * like ravening and roaring lions.

6   I am poured out like water, * and all My bones are racked.

7   And My Heart has become like wax * melting away within My bosom.

8   My throat is dried up like baked clay, * and My tongue cleaves to My jaws.

9   And they gave Me gall for My food, * and in My thirst they gave Me vinegar to drink.

10   And they brought Me down into the dust of death, * and added to the grief of My wounds.

11   I have slept and I have risen again, * and My most holy Father has received Me with glory.

12   Holy Father, You have held My right hand and have guided Me with Your counsel, * and with glory have lifted Me up.

13   For what else have I in heaven, * and apart from You what have I desired upon earth?

14   See, see, that I am God, says the Lord! * and I will be exalted among the nations and I will be exalted upon the earth.

15   Blessed be the Lord the God of Israel, Who has redeemed the souls of His servants by His own most precious Blood, * and will not abandon all who hope in Him.

16   And we know that he is coming, * for He will come to judge justice.

The Antiphon: *Holy Virgin Mary* in full.

At Vespers

1 All you peoples, clap your hands: * shout to God with cries of gladness!

2 For the Lord, the Most High, the awesome, * is the great King over all the earth.

3 Because the Most Holy Father of heaven, our King before all ages, * sent His beloved Son from on high, and has wrought salvation in the midst of the earth.

4 Let the heavens be glad and the earth rejoice; let the sea and all that fills it be moved; * let the plains be joyful and all things that are in them.

5 Sing to the Lord a new song; * sing to the Lord, all you lands!

6 For great is the Lord and highly to be praised: * awesome is He, beyond all gods.

7 Give to the Lord, you families of nations; give to the Lord glory and honor: * give to the Lord the glory due His name!

8 Offer your bodies and carry His holy Cross, * and follow to the very end His most holy precepts and commandments.

9 Let all the earth tremble before Him. * Say among the nations that the Lord has reigned from the Cross.

On the Feast of the Ascension add this verse (10):

10 And He ascended into heaven and is seated at the right hand of the most holy Father in heaven: be exalted above the heavens, O God; above all the earth be Your glory.

11 And we know that He is coming, * for He will come to judge justice.

The Antiphon *Holy Virgin Mary,* in full.

At Compline

The Antiphon: Holy Virgin Mary!

1   O God, I have declared to You my life; * My tears You have placed in Your sight.

2   All My enemies were devising evil against Me * and took counsel together.

3   They repaid Me evil for good, * and hatred for My love.

4   In return for My love they slandered Me, * but I gave Myself to prayer.

5   My Holy Father, King of heaven and earth, be not far from Me, * for distress is near, and there is no one to help Me.

6   May My enemies be turned back; * in whatever day I shall call upon You, behold I know You are My God.

7   My friends and My companions stand back because of My affliction, * and My neighbors stand afar off.

8   You have taken My friends away from Me: * You have made Me an abomination to them; I have been betrayed, and I cannot escape.

9   Holy Father, let Your help be not far from Me; * My God, come to My aid.

10 Make haste to help Me, O Lord, * the God of My salvation.

11 Glory to the Father, and to the Son, and to the Holy Spirit: As it was in the beginning, is now, and ever shall be, world without end. Amen!

The Antiphon *Holy Virgin Mary*, in full.

The concluding prayer to this Office at the end of Night Prayer is as follows:

Let us bless the Lord God living and true! Let us always render Him praise, glory, honor, blessing, and all good things!! Amen. Amen. So be it! So be it!

Part II

FRANCIS GUIDES
HIS BROTHERS

THE RULE OF 1221

Also called the Rule without a Papal Bull of approbation, or even the Second Rule. Saint Francis had obtained the approbation of the Order from Pope Innocent III in 1209 (or perhaps 1210), together with a brief Rule that has not survived as such, though we may suppose that the basic elements of that Rule are to be found in the present text, especially in the early chapters. Then as the Order grew, further guidelines needed for the friars were added to the primitive Rule, together with texts of Sacred Scripture which were the inspiration of many such regulations. Such texts of Scripture, we are told in The Chronicle of Friar Jordan of Giano *(n. 15), (which ends with the year 1262), were added by Brother Cesar of Speyer, a learned and holy man and a great preacher, who entered the Order while in the Holy Land (cf.* XIIIth Century Chronicles, *ed. P. Hermann, O.F.M., Chicago 1961, 30). Though this Rule did not receive Papal approval, its basic teachings are inculcated anew in the Rule of 1223. Hence it is of great importance in discovering the ideals and goals of Saint Francis, whose burning desire was to bring all men to Christ.*

THE RULE OF 1221

Prologue

1 In the Name of the Father and of the Son and of the Holy Spirit!

2. This is the life of the Gospel of Jesus Christ which Brother Francis asked of the Lord Pope to be granted and confirmed to him. And he conceded and confirmed it to him and to his brothers present and to come.

3. Brother Francis and whoever may be the head of this Order is to promise obedience and reverence to the Lord Pope Innocent and to his successors.

4. And all the other brothers are to be bound to obey Brother Francis and his successors.

[Chapter I. That the Brothers are to live without anything of their own and in chastity and obedience.]

1 The Rule and life of these brothers is this, namely to live in obedience, in chastity, and without anything of their own, and to follow the teaching and the footsteps of Our Lord Jesus Christ, who says: "If thou wilt be perfect, go and sell all that thou hast and give to the poor, and thou shalt have treasure in heaven; and come, follow Me" (Mt 19,21). And: "If any one will come after Me, let him deny himself and take up his cross and follow Me" (Mt 16, 24). In like manner: "If any one wishes to come to Me, and does not hate father and mother and wife and children and brothers and sisters, yes and his own life also, cannot be My disciple" (Lk 14, 26). — And: "Everyone who has left father and mother, brothers or sisters, wife or children, houses or lands for My sake, shall receive a hundred-fold and

shall possess life everlasting" (cf. Mt 19, 29; Mk 10, 29-30; Lk 18, 29).

[Chapter II. On the Reception and Clothing of the Brothers.]

1 If anyone wishing by divine inspiration to embrace this life should come to our Brothers, let him be received kindly by them.

2 And if he be firmly resolved to accept our life, let the Brothers take great care not to meddle with his temporal affairs, but present him as soon as possible to their Minister.

3 The Minister is to receive him kindly and encourage him and carefully explain to him the tenor of our life.

4 Thereupon, if he be willing and able, in conscience and without hindrance, he is to sell all his goods and endeavor to distribute them all to the poor.

5 The Brothers and the minister of the Brothers are to take care not to interfere in any way in his affairs,

6 nor are they to receive any money, either themselves or through a middle man.

7 If however they are in want, the Brothers can receive other material necessities, except money, by reason of their needs, like other poor people.

8 And when he has returned, the Minister is to give him the clothes of probation for a year, namely two tunics without a hood, and a cord, and breeches and a caperon [small round cape] reaching to the cord.

9 When the year and term of probation is ended, let him be received to obedience.

10 Thereafter it shall not be lawful for him to pass to another Order nor to "wander about beyond obedience", according to the command of the Lord Pope and the Gospel, for "no man putting his hand to the plow and looking back, is fit for the kingdom of God" (Lk 9, 62).

11 If however some one should come who cannot give away his goods without some difficulty, yet has the

spiritual will to do so, let him relinquish them, and this is sufficient for him.

12 No one is to be received contrary to the form and practice of Holy Church.

13 The other friars who have promised obedience are to have one tunic with a hood and another without a hood, if it should be necessary, and a cord and breeches.

14 And let all the Brothers be clothed in mean garments, which they may quilt with sackcloth and other pieces with the blessing of God, for the Lord says in the Gospel: "Those who are in costly apparel and live sumptuously" (cf. Lk 7, 25), and "who are clothed in soft garments, are in the houses of kings" (Mt 11, 8).

15 And though they may be called hypocrites, let them not cease to do good; and let them not seek costly clothes in this world, that they may have a garment in the kingdom of heaven.

[Chapter III. On the Divine Office and Fasting.]

1 The Lord says: "This kind" of demons "cannot go out save in fasting and prayer" (cf. Mk 9, 28);

2 and again: "When you fast, be not as the hypocrites, sad" (Mt 6, 16).

3 For this reason all the friars, whether clerics or laics, are to say the divine office, the praises and prayers, according to what they are assigned to say.

4 The clerics are to perform the office and say it for the living and the dead according to the custom of clerics.

5 And for any defect or negligence of the brothers, they are to say each day the *Misereri mei Deus* [Ps 50] together with the Our Father;

6 and for the deceased brothers, let them say the *De profundis* [Ps 129] with the *Pater Noster*.

7 And they may have only the books necessary to perform their office.

8 And the lay brothers who know how to read the psalter may also have one.

9 The others who do not know how to read may not have a book.

10 The lay friars are to say the "I believe in God" and twenty-four Our Fathers with the Glory to the Father for Matins; for Lauds, five; for Prime, the "I believe in God" and seven other Our Fathers with the Glory to the Father; for Tierce, Sext and Nones, for each hour, seven; for Vespers, twelve; for Compline, the "I believe in God", and seven Our Fathers with the Glory to the Father. For the dead, seven Our Fathers, with "Eternal Rest". And for any defect or negligence of the friars, three Our Fathers every day.

11 And in like manner all the friars are to fast from the feast of All Saints to the Nativity [Christmas] and from Epiphany, when Our Lord Jesus Christ began to fast, until Easter.

12 But at other times, according to this life, they are not bound to fast except on Fridays.

13 And they are allowed to eat of all foods that are placed before them, according to the Gospel (cf. Lk 10, 8).

[Chapter IV. On the Ministers and the others Friars: Their relationship.]

1 In the Name of the Lord!

2 All the Brothers who are appointed as ministers and servants of the other friars are to place their Brothers in the provinces and in the places where they may be; and should often visit them and admonish and strengthen them in the Spirit.

3 And all my other blessed Brothers are diligently to obey them in those things which have to do with the salvation of (their) soul and are not contrary to our life.

4 And let them act among themselves according to the word of the Lord: *Whatever you wish that others do to you, do you also to them* (Mt 7, 12), and:

5 *What you do not wish done to you, do not do it to others* (cf. Tob 4, 16).

6 The ministers and servants are to remember what the

Lord says: *I did not come to be served, but to serve* (Mt 20, 28); and that because the care of the souls of the friars is committed to them, if anything should be lost through their fault and bad example, they will have to render an account on judgement-day before the Lord Jesus Christ (cf. Mt 12, 36).

[Chapter V. On the Correction of the friars for an offence.]

1 Therefore take care of your souls and those of your Brothers, for "it is a fearful thing to fall into the hands of the living God" (Hebr 10, 31).

2 If however one of the ministers should give a command to one of the Brothers which would be against our life or against his conscience, he is not to be held to obey him; for that is not obedience in which a fault or sin is committed.

3 Let all the Brothers however who are under the ministers and servants reasonably and carefully weigh the actions of the ministers and servants.

4 And if they should see any of them walking according to the flesh and not according to the Spirit in keeping with the pattern of our life, if he has not amended after a third admonition, they are to denounce him in the Chapter of Pentecost to the Minister and Servant of the whole brotherhood, no matter what obstacle may be put in their way.

5 If however among the friars, wherever they are, there should be some brother who desires to live according to the flesh and not according to the Spirit, the Brothers with whom he is are to admonish, instruct and correct him with humility and love.

6 But if after a third admonition he does not wish to amend, as soon as they can they are to send him to his minister and servant, or to make the matter known to him; and the minister and servant is to do with him what may seem more expedient according to God.

7 All the friars, both the ministers and servants and the others, must take care not to be disturbed or angered

because of the sin or misdeed of another, because the devil seeks to corrupt many through the sin of one man.

8 Instead, in a spiritual way, as best they can, let them help the one who has sinned, for it is not *they who are in health* that *need a physician, but they who are sick* (Mt 9, 12; Mk 2, 17).

9 In like manner, none of the friars is to have any power or domination, especially among themselves, for,

10 as the Lord says in the Gospel: *The princes of the gentiles lord it over them; and those who are the greater exercise power over them* (Mt 20, 25). But so it shall not be among the friars.

11 And *whoever would be the greater among them should be their minister* (cf. Mt 20, 26) and servant;

12 and *he who is the greater* among them must *become as the lesser* (cf. Lk 22, 26).

13 And no brother is to do evil or speak evil to another;

14 much rather, *through the charity of the Spirit* they should willingly *serve* and obey *one another* (cf. Gal 5, 13; Vulgate).

15 And this is the true and holy obedience of Our Lord Jesus Christ.

16 And as often as they may have turned away from the commands of the Lord and wandered outside of obedience, as the Prophet says (cf. Ps 118, 21), let all the brothers recognize that they are cursed and outside of obedience as long as they would knowingly persist in such sin.

17 And when they shall have persevered in the commandments of the Lord which they promised by the Holy Gospel and their life, let them know that they abide in true obedience and are blessed by the Lord.

[Chapter VI. On the Recourse of the Brothers to their Ministers; and that no Brother is to be called Prior.]

1 In whatever places the Brothers are, if they cannot observe our life, they should have recourse as soon as possible to their Minister and make this known to him.

2　On his part, the Minister is to try to meet their needs as he himself would wish to have done for him if he were faced with a like situation.

3　And no one is to be called Prior, but all in general are to be called the Lesser Brothers [= Friars Minor].

4　And let one wash the feet of the other (cf. John 13, 14).

[Chapter VII. On the Manner of Serving and Working.]

1　All the Brothers in whatever places they may be among other people to serve or to labor, are not to be administrators nor chancery officials, nor are they to be overseers in the houses in which they are serving; nor are they to accept any office that may give rise to scandal or bring about the loss of one's soul (cf. Mk 8, 36).

2　Rather, let them be inferior [*minores*] and subject to all who are in the same house (cf. Testament, n. 19).

3　The Brothers who know how to work should work and continue the same trade which they have learned, if it be not against the wellbeing of the soul and they can exercise it honorably.

4　For the Prophet says: *You shall eat the labors of your fruits: blessed are you, and it shall be well with you* [Ps 127, 2, according to the Roman psalter].

5　And the Apostle says: *Who does not wish to work, let him not eat* (cf. II Thess 3, 10);

6　and: *Each should continue* in that craft and work that was his when he was called (cf I Cor 7, 24).

7　And for their work they can receive all things necessary except money.

8　And when need be, they may go for alms like other poor people.

9　And they may have the utensils and tools needed for their trades.

10　All the Brothers should diligently apply themselves to work, for it is written: "Be always busy in some good work, that the devil may find you occupied";

11　and again: "Idleness is the enemy of the soul" [St. Benedict, Rule, 48, 1].

12 For such reasons the servants of God must always be engaged in prayer or in some good work.

13 The Brothers are to take care that, wherever they may be, in hermitages or in other places, they do not appropriate any place to themselves or defend it against anyone.

14 And whoever may come to them, friend or foe, thief or robber, let him be received with kindness.

15 And wherever the friars are and in whatever place they meet, with spirit and love let them greet and honor one another without complaining (cf. I Peter 4, 9).

16 And let them take care not to appear outwardly as sad and gloomy hypocrites, but show they are joyful in the Lord (cf. Phil 4, 4), and merry and becomingly gracious (See Celano, Second Life of St. Francis, n. 128).

[Chapter VIII. That the Brothers are not to receive money.]

1 The Lord bids us the Gospel: *Take heed, beware of all malice and couvetousness* (cf. Lk 12, 15);

2 again: *Keep yourselves from worries of this world and from the cares of this life* (cf. Lk 21, 34).

3 Hence none of the Brothers, wherever he may be and wheresoever he goes, is to handle or receive money or coins or have it received, either for clothing or for books or as payment for any work, or indeed for any reason, except the manifest needs of the sick Brothers. For we must not think or imagine there is more value in coins and money than in stones.

4 And the devil seeks to blind those who desire money or value it more than stones.

5 Let us then who have left all things take care lest for so little we lose the kingdom of heaven.

6 And if in any place we should find coins, let us not have any more regard for them than for the dust we tread under our feet, for it is *vanity of vanities, and all is vanity* (Eccles 1, 2).

7 And if it should have happened, which God forbid, that some brother is collecting or has money or coins, save

only for the aforesaid needs of the sick, all the Brothers are to consider him a false brother and an apostate and a thief and robber and as having a purse (cf. John 12, 6 = Judas), unless he truly repents.

8 And in no way are the Brothers to receive money or have it received, nor are they to seek it or have it quested as an alms, nor coins [likewise], for any houses or places; neither are they to accompany anyone who is questing money or coins for such places.

9 All the other services which are not contrary to our life the Brothers can do in the "places" with the blessing of God.

10 When however the lepers are in manifest need, the Brothers can seek alms for them.

11 But let them be most wary of money.

12 In like manner let all the friars beware of traipsing through the world for any filthy lucre.

[Chapter IX. On Seeking Alms.]

1 All the Brothers are to strive to follow the humility and poverty of Our Lord Jesus Christ, and keep in mind that it behooves us to have nothing else in the whole world save that, as the Apostle says: *Having food and clothing, we have all that we need* (I Tim 6, 8).

2 And they should rejoice when they live among persons who are lowly and despised, among the poor and the weak and the sick and the lepers and the beggars by the wayside.

3 And when it should be necessary, let them go for alms.

4 And they should not be ashamed and rather recall to mind that Our Lord Jesus Christ, *the Son of the Living God* (John 11, 27), set His face like flint (Is 50, 7) and was not ashamed.

5 And he was poor and a stranger and lived on alms, Himself and the Blessed Virgin and His disciples.

6 And should people treat them with contempt and refuse to give them alms, let them thank God for this, because for such shameful treatment they shall receive great

honor before the judgment seat of Our Lord Jesus Christ.

7 And let them realize that such shame is to the discredit of those who inflict it, not of those who suffer it.

8 Moreover, an alms is an inheritance and a right which is due the poor, which Our Lord Jesus Christ gained for us.

9 And the Brothers who toil in seeking alms will have a great reward, and also procure and acquire a like reward for those who give the alms: for all that men leave behind them in this world will perish; but for the charity and the alms they have given they will receive a reward from God.

10 And without hesitation let one make known his need to his brothers, that he may find and minister what the other lacks.

11 And let each one love and care for his brother as a mother loves and cares for her child, in so far as God gives them the grace (cf. I Thess 2, 7; and the Final Rule, c. 6, n. 8).

12 And *the one who does not eat* [= is fasting] *must not sit in judgment on him who eats* (Rom 14, 3).

13 And whenever some [general] need should arise, it is to be lawful for all the Brothers wherever they may be to use all foods that men can eat, as the Lord said of David, who ate *the holy bread* (cf. Mt 12, 4) *which only the priests were permitted to eat* (Mk 2, 26).

14 And let them recall what the Lord says: *But take heed to yourselves lest perhaps your hearts be bloated with indulgence and drunkenness and the cares of this life, and that Day come upon you suddenly;*

15 *for like a snare it will come upon all who dwell on the face of the whole earth* (Lk 21, 34-35).

16 In like manner also, in a time of manifest necessity all the Brothers may do as best they can, as the Lord shall give them grace: for necessity has no law.

[Chapter X. Of the Brothers who are sick.]

1 If any of the Brothers should fall sick, wherever he may be, the other friars are not to leave him unless one of the Brothers, or more if need be, is chosen who will serve him as they would wish to be served themselves.

2 But in extreme necessity they can commit him to some person to take care of him in his infirmity.

3 And I ask the friar who is sick, to give thanks to the Creator for all things; and to desire to be whatever the Lord wills him to be, whether well or sick, for all whom God has destined for life eternal (cf. Acts 13, 48) He instructs by the rod of afflictions and infirmities and by the spirit of compunction, as the Lord says: *Those whom I love I correct and chastise* (cf. Apoc 3, 19).

4 And if anyone is disturbed or angry either against God or against the Brothers, or perhaps has asked too solicitously for medicines in too much of a desire to free his body, which is soon to die and is the enemy of the soul: this reaction comes to him from the Evil One, and (such a Brother) is carnal and does not seem to belong to the friars, because he loves his body more than the soul.

[Chapter XI. That the Brothers are not to speak evil [of others] or complain, but are to love one another.]

1 And all the Brothers are to be careful not to calumniate anyone or to contend in words (cf. 2 Tim 2, 14).

2 Rather, let them strive to maintain silence whenever God gives them the grace.

3 Nor should they dispute among themselves or with others; instead, they are to seek to answer humbly, saying: "I am an unprofitable servant" (cf. Lk 17, 10).

4 And they must not be angry, because *everyone who is angry with his brother shall be liable to judgment; whoever shall say to his brother Raca shall be in danger of the council; and whosoever shall say: Thou fool, shall be in danger of hell-fire* (cf. Mt 5, 22).

5 And let them love one another as the Lord says: *This is My commandement: love one another as I have loved you* (John 15, 21).

6 And by their works let them show the love they have for each other, as the Apostle says: *Let us not love in word or in tongue, but in deed and in truth* (I John 3, 18).

7 And *they are not to speak evil of anyone* (Titus 3, 2);

8 or grumble, or slander others, for it is written: *Gossips and slanderers are hateful to God* (cf. Rom 1, 29-30).

9 And they must be gentle, *showing all courtesy toward all men* (Titus 3, 2),

10 not judging and not condemning.

11 Moreover, as the Lord says, let them not stare at the slight offences of others (cf. Mt 7, 3; Lk 6, 41),

12 but rather *recount their own in the bitterness of their soul* (Is 38, 15).

13 And let them *strive to enter by the narrow gate* (Lk 13, 24), for the Lord tells us: *Narrow is the gate and rough the road that leads to life; and few there are who find it* (Mt 7, 14).

[Chapter XII. On unbecoming Glances and the Company of Women.]

1 All the Brothers, wherever they are or may go, are to avoid unbecoming glances and the company of women.

2 And none is to counsel them [alone] or walk alone with them or eat out of the same dish with them at table.

3 The priests are to speak to them uprightly when giving a penance or other spiritual counsel.

4 And no woman is ever to be received to obedience by any friar; but once he has given her advice, she is to do penance wherever she wills.

5 And let us all keep careful watch over ourselves and keep our members clean, for the Lord says: *Anyone who looks lustfully at a woman has already committed adultery with her in his heart* (Mt 5, 28).

6 And the Apostle [says]: *Do you not know that your members are the temple of the Holy Spirit?* (I Cor 6,

19). Hence whoever *violates the temple of God, him shall God destroy* (I Cor 3, 17).

[Chapter XIII. On Avoiding Fornication.]

1 If any of the Brothers at the instigation of the devil should commit fornication, he is to be stripped of the habit which he lost by his base iniquity, hand it over completely, and be altogether expelled from our religion [= Order].

2 And thereafter let him do penance for his sins.

[Chapter XIV. How the Brothers are to go through the World.]

1 When the Brothers go through the world they are to carry nothing for the journey, neither a sack, nor scrip, nor bread, nor money, nor staff.

2 And into whatever house they may enter, let their first greeting be: *Peace be to this house* (Lk 10, 5).

3 And as long as they stay in that house they may eat and drink such things as they [their hosts] may have.

4 They should offer no resistance to injury (cf. Mt 5, 39); indeed, if someone slaps them on one cheek, they should offer him the other as well (Mt 5, 39; Lk 6, 29).

5 And if one takes their cloak, let them not hang on to their tunic.

6 Let them give to everyone who begs from them; and if some one carries off things that belong to them, they should not demand them back (Lk 6, 30).

[Chapter XV. That the Brothers are not to ride horseback.]

1 I enjoin on all my Brothers, both clerics and laics, who go through the world or reside in places [= houses, hermitages, caves, etc.], that in no wise they have any beast of burden in their places or entrusted to others or in any other way.

2 Nor it is lawful for them to ride horseback unless they are constrained by infirmity or great necessity.

[Chapter XVI. Of the Brothers who go among the Saracens and other Infidels.]

1 The Lord says: *Behold I send you as sheep in the midst of wolves.*

2 *Be therefore wise as serpents and simple as doves* (Mt 10, 16).

3 Hence any Brother who may wish to go among the Saracens and other unbelievers may go with the permission of his minister and servant.

4 And the minister is to give them permission and not stand in their way if he sees they are fit to be sent: for he will be held to render an account to the Lord if in this or in other things he has acted indiscreetly.

5 On their part, the Brothers who go may live among them in the Spirit in two ways.

6 One way is this, that they do not stir up disputes or contentions, but *be subject to every human creature for God's sake* (I Peter 2, 13), and acknowledge that they are Christians.

7 The other way is that when they see it pleases the Lord, they proclaim the word of God, that they should believe in God the Father Almighty, the Son and the Holy Spirit, the Creator of all things, the Son Who is the Redeemer and Savior; and that they should be baptized and become Christians, because whoever is *not born again of water and the Holy Spirit cannot enter the Kingdom of God* (Jn 3, 5).

8 These and other things which please God they may say to them and to others, because the Lord says in the Gospel: *Whoever shall acknowledge Me before men, I will also acknowledge him before My Father who is in heaven* (Mt 10, 32).

9 Again: *He that shall be ashamed of Me and of My words, the Son of Man will be ashamed of him when He shall come in His glory and that of His Father and His angels* (cf. Lk 9, 26).

10 And all the Brothers, wherever they are, must remember that they have given themselves and handed over their

bodies to the Lord Jesus Christ.

11 And for love of Him they must expose themselves to enemies both seen and unseen; for the Lord says: *Whoever shall lose his life for Me will save it unto life eternal* (Lk 9, 24; Mt 25, 46).

12 *Blessed are they who suffer persecution for justice' sake, for theirs is the kingdom of heaven* (Mt 5, 10).

13 *If they have persecuted Me, they will also persecute you* (Jo 15, 20).

14 And again: *If they persecute you in one city, flee into another* (cf. Mt 11, 23).

15 *Blessed are you when men shall hate you and speak evil of you, and persecute you and ostracize you and insult you and cast out your name as evil, and utter every kind of slander against you because of Me* (Mt 5, 11, and Lk 6, 22).

16 *Be glad on that day and rejoice* (Lk, 6, 23),

17 for your reward is great in heaven (cf. Mt 5, 12). *And I say to you who are My friends: Do not be afraid of them* (Lk 12, 4).

18 *And do not fear those who kill the body* (Mt 10, 8) *and thereafter can do no more* (Lk 12, 4).

19 *See that you be not troubled* (Mt 24, 6), *for in your patient endurance you shall possess your souls* (Lk 21, 19).

20 And *whoever holds out to the end will be saved* (Mt 10, 22; 24, 13).

[Chapter XVII. On Preachers.]

1 No Brother is to preach in a manner contrary to the laws of the Church or without the permission of his Minister.

2 And let the Minister take care not to grant such permission indiscreetly to any one.

3 All the Brothers, however, are to preach by their works.

4 And no Minister or preacher is to consider the care of the Brothers or the office of preaching as something to which he has a right. Rather, at whatever hour he is bidden, let him give up his office without any opposition.

5 Wherefore in the charity which God is (I Jo 4, 16) I beseech all my Brothers, preachers, orators, workers, both clerics and laics, that they strive to humble themselves in all things,

6 and not to glory or rejoice in themselves or inwardly to pride themselves by reason of the good words and works, or indeed of any good, which God sometimes does or says and works in them and through them, in keeping with what the Lord says: *Yet rejoice not in this, that spirits* [devils] *are subject to you* (Lk 10, 20).

7 And let us know for certain that nothing belongs to us save vices and sins.

8 And we ought rather to rejoice when we would fall *into every sort of trial* (Jas 1, 2), and would have to put up with all kinds of afflictions or tribulations of soul or body in this world for the sake of life eternal.

9 Let all of us Brothers guard against all pride and vainglory,

10 and keep ourselves from the wisdom of this world and the prudence of the flesh (Rom 8, 6).

11 For the prompting of the flesh seeks and strives to be full of talk, but cares little for action;

12 and seeks not God-centeredness [Latin: religion] and holiness in the inner man, but looks for and desires a religiosity and holiness that can be seen by men.

13 And it is of these that the Lord says: *Amen, I say to you, they have received their reward* (Mt 6, 2).

14 The Spirit of the Lord, on the other hand, wishes the outer man [the flesh] to be mortified and despised and considered mean and of little worth;

15 and strives instead for humility and patience and for the pure and simple and true peace of the inner man [the spirit]

16 And always and above all else it longs for divine fear and divine wisdom and the divine love of the Father and the Son and the Holy Spirit.

17 And let us render all good things to the Lord God most high and supreme, and acknowledge that all good things are His, and give Him thanks for all from Whom all

good things come.

18 And may He, the most High and Supreme, the only true God, have, and may there be rendered to Him and may He receive all honor and reverence, all praises and blessings, all thanks and glory, to whom every good belongs, who alone is good (cf. Lk 18, 19).

19 And when we see or hear evil said or done, or God blasphemed, let us say well and do well and praise God (cf. Rom 12, 21), *who is blessed forever* (Rom 1, 25).

[Chapter XVIII. How the Ministers are to meet together.]

1 Every year each Minister may convene with his friars wherever it may please them on the Feast of Saint Michael the Archangel, to treat of those things which belong to God.

2 For all the ministers who are in parts beyond the sea [the Mediterranean] and beyond the mountains [the Alps] once in three years, and the other Ministers once each year, are to come to the Chapter of Pentecost at the church of Saint Mary of the Porziuncola, unless it be otherwise ordained by the Minister and Servant of the whole brotherhood.

[Chapter XIX. That the Brothers are to live in a Catholic manner.]

1 All the Brothers are to be Catholics and live and speak in keeping with their belief.

2 Should anyone of them, however, have erred from the faith and the Catholic way of life in word or in deed and has not amended, he is to be altogether expelled from our brotherhood.

3 And we are to regard all clerics and all religious as masters in the things that regard the salvation of souls and do not deviate from our religion; and we are to hold in reverence their order and office and administration in the Lord.

[Chapter XX. On [the sacrament of] Penance and the Reception of the Body and Blood of Our Lord Jesus Christ.]

1 And my blessed Brothers, both clerics and laics, are to confess their sins to priests of our religion [= Order].

2 And if they cannot, let them confess to other discreet and Catholic priests, knowing full well and consciously that from whichever Catholic priests they receive penance and absolution they will, beyond all doubt, be absolved of their sins if they take care to carry out humbly and faithfully the penance enjoined on them.

3 Should they not be able to find a priest at that moment, let them confess to one of their Brothers, as the Apostle James tells us: *Confess your sins to one another* (Jas 5, 16).

4 Yet on this account let them not fail to have recourse to a priest, since the power of binding and loosing is given only to priests.

5 And thus contrite and confessed let them receive the Body and Blood of Our Lord Jesus Christ with great humility and veneration, mindful that the Lord says: *He who eats My flesh and drinks My blood has life eternal* (cf. Jo 6, 54); and: *Do this as a remembrance of Me* (Lk 22, 19).

[Chapter XXI. On the Praise and Exhortation which all the Brothers may make.]

1 And this or a like exhortation and praise all my Brothers, whenever it may please them, can announce among any and all men with the blessing of God:

2 Fear and honor, praise and bless,
   Give thanks to, and adore,
   The Lord God Almighty, in Trinity and Unity,
   Father, Son and Holy Spirit: Creator of all.

3 Do penance! (Mt 3, 2)
   Bring forth worthy fruits of penance for we shall soon die!.

4 *Give, and it shall be given to you* (Lk 6, 38).

5 *Pardon, and you shall be pardoned* (Lk 6, 37).

6 And *if you do not forgive men their sins* (Mt 6, 14), the Lord will not forgive you your sins (Mk 11, 25); Confess all your sins! (cf. Jas 5, 16).

7 Blessed are those who die in penance, for they will be in the kingdom of heaven.

8 Woe to those who do not die in penance,
For they will be the children of the devil whose works they do (cf. Jo 8, 41), and they shall go into the everlasting fire.

9 Take care and abstain from every evil and persevere unto the end in the good.

[Chapter XXII. On the Admonition of the Brothers.]

1 Let all us Brothers be mindful that the Lord says: *Love your enemies and do good to those who hate you* (Mt 5, 44),

2 because Our Lord Jesus Christ, whose footsteps we must follow (cf. I Pet 2, 21), called His betrayer "friend" (cf. Mt 26, 50) and readily offered Himself to those who crucified Him.

3 Our friends therefore are all those who unjustly inflict on us tribulations and anguish, shame and injuries, sorrows and torments, martyrdom and death. 4 We must have great love for them since from what they inflict upon us we have life eternal.

5 And let us hate our body with its vices and sins; because by [our] living according to the flesh this devil wishes to deprive us of the love of Jesus Christ and of eternal life and to cast itself with all else into hell;

6 for by our own fault we are foul-smelling, wretched, and opposed to what is good, but prompt and open to what is evil because, as the Lord says in the Gospel:

7 From the heart sprout and come forth evil thoughts, adulteries, fornications, murders, thefts, avarice, wickedness, guile, lewdness, the evil eye, false testimonies, blasphemy, foolishness (Mt 15, 19-20; see

Mk 7, 22-23).

8   All these evils come from within, from the heart of man *and these are the things that defile a man* (Mt 15, 19-20; cf. Mk 7, 22-23).

9   But now, having left the world behind, we have nothing else to do save to follow the will of the Lord and to please Him.

10 Let us be most careful that we be not the ground along the path or that which is stony or full of thorns, according to what the Lord says in the Gospel:

11 *The seed is the word of God* (Lk 8, 11).

12 That however which *fell by the wayside and was trodden down* (Lk 8, 5) *are those who hear* (Lk 8, 12) the word and do not understand.

13 And *immediately the devil comes and steals away* what was sown in their hearts and takes the word out of their hearts lest they believe and be saved (Lk 8, 12).

14 That which fell on rocky ground are those who when they have heard the word, immediately accept it with joy.

15 But when tribulation and persecution come because of the word, they soon falter (Mt 13, 21). And such have no root in them, except briefly, for they believe for a while, but fall away in time of temptation (Lk 8, 13).

16 The seed that fell among briars are those who hear the word of God, but anxiety and the cares of this world and the lure of riches and cravings of other sorts come to choke the word and it bears no yield (Mk 4, 19).

17 *What was sown on good ground are those who in a good and perfect heart, on hearing the word,* understand *and keep it and bring forth fruit in patience* (Lk 8, 15).

18 And for this reason we Brothers, as the Lord says, should *let the dead bury their dead* (Mt 8, 22).

19 And let us be much on our guard against the malice and cunning of Satan, whose desire it is that man not center his mind and heart on God.

20 And roaming about, he seeks to seduce the heart of man under pretext of some reward or benefit, and to choke

out the words and precepts of the Lord from our memory, and desires to blind the heart of man by worldly affairs and care, and make his dwelling therein.

21 This is what the Lord tells us: *When an unclean spirit departs from a man, it roams through dry and waterless wastes in search of a place to rest;*

22 *and finding none, it says: I will go back to my house which I left.*

23 *And coming, it finds it empty, swept clean, and tidied* (Mt 12, 44).

24 *And it goes out and returns with seven other spirits far worse than itself, and they enter in and dwell there: and the last state of that man is worse than all that went before* (Lk 11, 26).

25 For this reason, Brothers all, let us be always on our guard lest under pretext of some gain or activity or help we lose or turn our mind and heart away from the Lord.

26 But in that holy charity which God is, I beg all my Brothers, both the ministers and the others, that, overcoming every obstacle and putting aside all care and worry, as best they can, they strive to serve, love, honor and adore the Lord God with clean heart and pure mind, which He seeks above all.

27 And let us always make within us a dwelling-place and abode for Him who is the Lord God almighty, Father, Son, and Holy Spirit, who says: *Be on the watch, praying constantly, that you may be accounted worthy to escape whatever is to come, and stand secure before the Son of Man* (Lk 21, 36).

28 *And when you stand to pray, say: Our Father, who art in heaven* (Mk 11, 25; Mt 6, 9).

29 And let us adore Him with a pure heart, for of necessity we must *pray always and not lose heart* (Lk 18, 1),

30 for the Father seeks such worshipers (Jo, 4, 23).

31 *God is Spirit, and those who worship Him must worship Him in Spirit and in truth* (Jo 4, 24).

32 And let us hasten back to Him as to *the Shepherd and Guardian of our souls* (I Pet 2, 25), who says: *I am the*

Good Shepherd who feed My sheep, and I lay down My life for My sheep (ancient Easter antiphon, now at Morning Prayer, fourth week of the Easter cycle).

33 *All you are brothers;*
34 *and do not call anyone on earth your father; for One is your Father, who is in heaven.*
35 *And do not be called teachers: for One is your Teacher, who is in heaven* (cf. Mt 23, 8-10).
36 *If you abide in me, and My words stay part of you, you shall ask whatever you will, and it will be done for you* (Jo 15, 7).
37 *Wherever two or three are gathered in My name, there am I in their midst* (Mt 19, 20).
38 *Behold, I am with you even to the end of the world* (Mt 28, 20).
39 *The words I have spoken to you are spirit and life* (Jo 6, 64).
40 *I am the Way, and the Truth, and the Life* (Jo 14, 6).
41 Let us then hold fast the words, the life, the teaching, and the Holy Gospel of Him who deigned to pray to the Father for us and to manifest His Name also to us, saying: *Father, glorify Your Name* (Jo 12, 28); and: *Give glory to Your Son that Your Son may give glory to You* (Jo 17, 1).
42 *Father, I have made Your Name known to the men whom You gave Me* (Jo 17, 6); for *the message You entrusted to Me I have entrusted to them; and they received it and have known that I came from You, and have believed it was You who sent Me.*
43 *For these I pray, not for the world,*
44 *but for these You have given Me, for they are Yours, just as all that belongs to Me is Yours* (Jo 17, 8-10).
45 *Holy Father, keep them in Your Name whom You have given Me: that they may be one, as We also are* (Jo 17, 11).
46 *I say this while still in the world, that they may have [My] joy in them.*
47 *I gave them Your word, and the world has hated them because they are not of this world, as I also am not of*

the world.

48 *I do not ask You to take them out of the world, but to guard them from the evil one* (Jo 17, 13-15).

49 Make *them* wondrous *in the truth.*

50 *Your word is truth.*

51 *As You have sent Me into the world, so I have sent them into the world.*

52 *For their sakes I consecrate Myself now, that they may be consecrated in truth.*

53 *I do not pray for them alone, but for those* [also] *who will believe in Me* because of *their word* (cf. Jo 17, 16-20), *that their union may be complete, and the world may know that You sent Me and that You loved them as You loved Me* (Jo 17, 23).

54 *And I will make known Your name to them, that the love with which You loved Me may be in them, and I in them* (cf. Jo 17, 26).

55 *Father, all those You gave Me I would that where I am they also may be with Me that they may see Your glory in Your kingdom!* Amen! (Jo 17, 24; Mt 20, 21).

[Chapter XXIII. A Prayer and Thanksgiving.]

1 Almighty, Most Holy, Most High and Sovereign God, Holy and Just Father, Lord, king of heaven and earth, for Your own sake we give thanks to You that by Your holy will and through Your only Son with the Holy Spirit You have created all things spiritual and corporal; and *placed* us, who are *made to Your image and likeness, in Paradise* (cf. Gen 1, 26; 2, 15).

2 And we have fallen by our own fault.

3 And we give You thanks that as through Your Son You created us, so through Your holy love with which You loved us You caused Him to be born true God and true Man of the glorious ever-virgin most blessed holy Mary, and willed that by His Cross and Blood and Death we captives be redeemed.

4 And we give thanks to You because Your very Son is to come in the glory of His majesty to send the wicked,

who have not done penance and have not known You, into eternal fire, and to say to all who have known and adored You and served You in penance: *Come, you blessed of My Father! Receive the kingdom which has been prepared for you from the beginning of the world* (Mt 25, 34).

5 And because all us wretches and sinners are not worthy to name You, we humbly pray that Our Lord Jesus Christ, Your beloved Son on whom Your favor rested (cf. Mt 17, 5), together with the Holy Spirit the Advocate, give thanks to You as it pleases You and Him for everthing. He suffices You always for all, through Whom You have done such great things for us! Alleluja!

6 And for love of You we humbly beseech the glorious Mother, the most blessed Mary ever virgin, Blessed Michael, Gabriel and Raphael, and all the choirs of the blessed seraphim, cherubim, thrones, dominations, principalities, powers, virtues, angels and archangels, Blessed John the Baptist, John the Evangelist, Peter, Paul, and the blessed patriarchs, the prophets, the Innocents, Apostles, Evangelists, disciples, martyrs, confessors, virgins, the blessed Elias and Enoch, and all the Saints, who were and will be and are, that, as it pleases You, for all these things they give thanks to You the Most High true God, eternal and living, with Your most dear Son Our Lord Jesus Christ, and with the Holy Spirit the Paraclete, forever and ever. Amen! Alleluja!

7 And all those within the holy Catholic and Apostolic Church who strive to serve the Lord God, and all the following orders: priests, deacons, subdeacons, acolytes, exorcists, lectors, ostiaries [doorkeepers], and all clerics, all religious men and women, all lay-brothers, and children, the poor and the needy, kings and princes, laborers and farmers, servants and masters, all virgins and the continent and married women, lay people, men and women, all infants, adolescents, young folk and old, healthy and sick, all little ones and the great, and all peoples, races, tribes and tongues, all nations and all

people the world over, who are and shall be, we humbly ask and beseech, all we Friars Minor, *useless servants* (Lk 17, 10), that we may all persevere in the true faith and in penance, for otherwise no one can be saved.

8 Let us all love with whole heart, with whole soul, with all mind, with all strength and fortitude, with whole intellect, with all powers, with all our might and whole affection, from the depths of our being, with all our desires and wills, the Lord God, who gave and gives to all of us our whole body, our whole soul, our whole life. He alone has done and does all good things for us who are such miserable beings, and wretched, putrid and unclean, ungrateful and evil.

9 Let us therefore desire nothing else, wish for nothing else; and let nothing else please and delight us, save our Creator, Redeemer and Savior, the only true God, who is the fullness of good, every good, all good, the true and highest Good; who alone is good (cf. Lk 18, 19), merciful, kind, gentle and sweet; who alone is holy, just, true, holy and upright; who alone is benign, pure, clean; from Him and through Him and in Him is all pardon, all grace, all glory of all the penitents and of the just and of the blessed who rejoice together in heaven.

10 Let nothing therefore impede us, nothing separate us, nothing stand in our way.

11 Let all of us everywhere, in every place, at every hour, and every season, daily and constantly, truly and humbly believe and hold in our hearts, and love, honor, adore, serve, praise and bless, glorify and exalt, magnify and render thanks to the most High and Supreme Eternal God, Trinity and Unity, the Creator of all and the Savior of all who believe and hope in Him and love Him who, without beginning and without end, is unchangeable, unseen, indescribable, ineffable, incomprehensible, unfathomable, blessed, praiseworthy, glorious, exalted above all, sublime, most high, gentle, lovable, delightful and wholly desirable above all else, for ever. Amen.

[Chapter XXXIV. Conclusion.]

1 In the Name of the Lord! I beseech all the Brothers that
they learn the tenor and sense of the things that are
written in this life [= the Rule] for the salvation of our
soul, and frequently recall them to mind.

2 And I earnestly beseech God that He who is omnipotent, Three and One, bless all who teach, learn, hold,
remember and fulfill these things, as often as they recall
and do what things are written here for the salvation of
our soul.

3 And, kissing their feet, I entreat all to love greatly, to
keep and to treasure (these things).

4 And on the part of Almighty God and of the Lord
Pope, and by obedience, I, Brother Francis, firmly command and enjoin that of the things that are written in
this Life no one shall subtract or add. Nor shall the
Brothers have any other Rule.

5 Glory to the Father and to the Son and to the Holy
Spirit, as it was in the beginning, is now and ever shall
be, world without end. Amen.

A LETTER TO A CERTAIN MINISTER

A beautiful portrait of the patience a minister (superior) is to have when confronted by the sins of a confrere. The Letter is to be dated as after the Rule of 1221, since this Rule does speak of mortal sins, in some eight or nine chapters; and before the definitive Rule of 1223. Chapter VII of this latter Rule treats of "the penance to be imposed on friars who sin". The text itself reads: "If any of the friars at the instigation of the enemy should sin mortally concerning those sins for which it has been ordained among the brothers that recourse be had to the provincial ministers only, etc.".
This is an interesting example of the development of legislation within the Order.

A LETTER TO A CERTAIN MINISTER

1 To Brother N., minister: May the Lord bless you!

2 I speak to you as best I can, on what concerns your soul: that those things which impede you from loving the Lord God and whoever has proved a hindrance, whether friars or others, even if they were to beat you, all such things you must reckon as a grace.

3 And so you should desire, and not something else.

4 And this should be for you as true obedience from the Lord God and from me, for I know surely that this is true obedience.

5 And love those who do these things to you.

6 And do not wish aught else from them, save in so far as the Lord may have granted you.

7 And in this love them; and do not wish that [for you] they be better Christians.

8 And let this be for you of more value than any hermitage.

9 And in this I seek to know if you love the Lord and me, His servant and yours, if you would do this: that there would not be any brother in the world who may have sinned to the utmost degree possible, that once he has looked into your eyes, would ever go away without your mercy, if he is seeking mercy.

10 And if he were not looking for mercy, you should ask him if he desires mercy.

11 And if a thousand times thereafter he should sin before your eyes, love him more than me, for this, that you may draw him to the Lord; and ever be merciful with such as these.

12 And this you should tell the guardians [local superiors], when you can, that for yourself you are determined to act thus.

13 Of all the chapters which are in the Rule which speak of mortal sins, with the help of God and the counsel of the friars in the Chapter of Pentecost we shall make such a chapter as this:

14 "If any brother at the instigation of the enemy shall have sinned mortally, he is to be bound by obedience to have recourse to his Guardian" [cf the final Rule of 1223, c.7].

15 And all the friars who might know that he has sinned are not to cause him shame or slander him; instead, they are to show great mercy towards him and keep most secret the sin of their brother, for *those who are well have no need of a physician, but those who are sick* (Mt 9, 12).

16 In like manner, they are bound by obedience to send him to his *custos* [= regional superior] with a companion.

17 The custos himself is to care for him with the mercy he would wish to receive if he were in a like situation.

18 And if a friar should have fallen into a venial sin, let him confess to his brother who is a priest.

19 And if there should be no priest at hand, let him confess

to his brother until he find a priest who will absolve him canonically, as was said above.

20 And these [non-priests?] are not to have any power to enjoin any other penance but this: *Go and sin no more* (cf. Jo 8, 11).

21 That this letter may be better observed, keep it with you until Pentecost when [at Chapter] you will be with your friars.

22 And these and all other things that are not clear in the Rule, with the help of the Lord God you [friars in chapter] will take care to complete.

THE FINAL RULE OF THE FRIARS MINOR

The Rule of 1221 was much more of a spiritual document than a piece of legislation. Hence it was hardly the type of Rule which seems to have been in favor in the thirteenth century: brief and to the point, combining both spirit and practice, ideals and legislation. Yet a careful examination of that Rule and the final Rule of 1223 reveals a substantial identity in defining and describing the life Saint Francis sought to follow, the life he proposed to his brothers as their inspiration and guide in following the Holy Gospel of Our Lord Jesus Christ.

Lacking indeed are the texts of Sacred Scripture selected by Cesar of Speyer, save for the most fundamental. On the other hand, in almost every chapter there are many more personal exhortations and commands on the part of Saint Francis. Undoubtedly he had the help of Cardinal Hugolino and of some learned friars; nonetheless, the Rule of 1223 is his in every way, in topics emphasized, in structure, phrasing, above all in spirit. The Introduction of Pope Honorius (before Chapter I) and the conclusion (after Chapter XII) are formulas or formalities used in the chancery of the Roman Curia, as is evident from a document of the year 1202, wherein the identical formulas are used by Pope Innocent III (cf. Patrologia lat. *217, 92 B-D).*

THE FINAL RULE OF THE FRIARS MINOR

1. In the name of the Lord
begins the manner of life
of the Friars Minor!

The Rule and Life of the Friars Minor is this: to observe the Holy Gospel of our Lord Jesus Christ through a life in obedience, without anything of their own, and in chastity. Brother Francis promises obedience and reverence to the Lord Pope Honorius and to his lawful successors, and to the Roman Church. And the other friars are to be bound to give obedience to Brother Francis and to his successors.

2. Of those who would embrace this Life
and how they should be received

Should any persons come to the friars with the desire to adopt this way of life, they are to be directed to their Ministers provincial. Only to the latter and to none other may the power be granted to receive new brethren. On their part, let the ministers subject such persons to a most careful examination on the Catholic faith and the Sacraments of the Church. They must be found to have true belief in all these matters, and the firm intention to profess loyally what they believe and steadfastly to conform their whole life long to such beliefs. Furthermore, they must not be married; or, if they are married, then their wives must either already have entered a monastery or, with the authority of the bishop of the diocese, have given their consent and themselves have taken a vow of continence; moreover, in this latter instance, the wives must be of such an age as to place them above suspicion.

If these requirements are fulfilled, the ministers are to tell them in the words of the Holy Gospel, to go and sell all that belongs to them and arrange to distribute them to the poor. Should they be unable to do this, it will suffice if they have the good will. But let the friars and their ministers keep themselves from any interest in the temporal affairs of the candidates, so that the latter are free to do with their goods whatever the Lord may inspire them. Yet if they stand in need of counsel, the ministers may have leave to refer them to some godfearing persons who may advise them how to give what they have to the poor.

When all this has been done, they are to give them the clothing worn during the year of probation, that is, two tunics without hoods, a cord, knee-breeches and a little cape that reaches to the cord. In this matter, however, the ministers may make other provisions if at some time it seems right to them according to the will of God.

When the year of probation is ended, they are to be received to obedience, whereby they will promise always to live according to this way and rule of life.

And by no manner or means shall they be allowed to leave this Order, both because the Pope has forbidden them and because according to the Holy Gospel: "No one, having put his hand to the plow and looking back, is fit for the kingdom of God". And those who have already promised obedience are to have one tunic with a hood; and, if they wish, a second without a hood. And those who are in need thereof may wear shoes. And all the friars are to wear clothing inferior in quality and appearance; and with the blessing of God they may quilt them with pieces of sack or other material.

I caution the friars and beg them not to look down upon or pass judgment on those people whom they see wearing soft and colorful garments and enjoying the choicest food and drink. Instead, each must criticize and despise himself.

3. On the Divine Office, and fasting,
and the way the friars should act among men

The clerics are to recite the Divine Office in accordance with
the rite of the Holy Church of Rome, with the exception of
the Psalter; and they may accordingly have breviaries. The
lay-friars, however, are to pray twenty-four Our Fathers for
Matins; five for Lauds; for Prime, Tierce, Sext and Nones,
seven for each of these; for Vespers, twelve; for Compline,
seven; and let them also pray for the dead.

They are to keep a fast during the time between All Saints'
Day and Christmas. The forty-day fast after the feast of the
Epiphany, a blessed season made sacred by the holy fasting
of the Lord Himself, those may observe who wish, and may
the Lord bless them for it; while those who do not wish to
keep it shall not be bound thereto. But they must keep the
other fast before the Feast of the Resurrection of the Lord.
Apart from these times, they are bound to fast only on
Fridays. But whenever there is a clear necessity, they need
not do any corporal fasting.

But I counsel my friars, warn and beseech them in the Lord
Jesus Christ, that when they go among other men in the
world they do not quarrel or bicker or criticize others.
Rather, it is their duty to be mild, peaceful and unassuming,
calm and humble; and their words, no matter with whom
they are speaking, must always be respectful of the other
person. And they are not to ride horseback, save when re-
quired by evident necessity or infirmity. Into whatever house
they enter, let them first say: "Peace to this house". And
according to the Holy Gospel, they are free to eat of
whatever food is set before them.

4. That the Friars are never to take Money

I strictly command the friars, each and all, never under any
circumstances to take money, whether it be in the form of
coins or of gold, either directly themselves or through some
person acting as intermediary. But for the needs of the sick

and for the clothing of the other friars, it shall be the duty of the ministers and custodes, and theirs alone, to turn to spiritual friends and with their help to provide what is needed. In this they will take into account the circumstances which can arise from such things as the diversity of places, the season of the year, and the cold climate. They may do whatever they feel is called for by the necessity, but always with the one condition made above, that they do not receive money in any form.

5. How the Friars are to Work

Those Brothers who are blessed by the Lord with ability in some form of work, should do their work faithfully and out of a sense of dedication. In this way they will put to rout that enemy of the soul, idleness; and at the same time not destroy the spirit of holy prayer and devotedness. For to this inner spirit all other things of life should positively contribute. As pay for their work, they may receive things needed for bodily sustenance, for themselves or their brethren, but not money in any form. In this let them act in all humility, as befits men who are the servants of God and followers of most holy poverty.

6. The Friars are not to acquire anything as their own.
They are to depend on Alms
The Care of the Sick Friars

The Friars are to take nothing as their own, whether it be a house, or a place, or anything at all. Instead, they are to be as pilgrims and strangers in this world; and as those who serve the Lord in poverty and lowliness, let them go begging for alms with full hope in Him. Nor should they feel shame thereby, since for our sakes the Lord himself came into this world as a poor man. Such indeed is the greatness of this perfect poverty that it makes you, my dearest brothers, heirs and kings of the kingdom of heaven, so that though you are thereby in want of this world's goods you are made rich in virtues. Let this always be your 'portion' here below, for it will bring you to 'the land of the living'. Hold fast to it, most beloved Brothers, with all your soul, and never desire to have aught else under heaven, for the sake of our Lord Jesus Christ. (Cf. Psalm 142, 6)

And wherever the friars may be together or come upon any of their brethren, let them show by their behavior toward one another that they are all of one family. And if one of them is in need, he should in full freedom and trust make known that need to the other. For if a mother has such care and love for the child born of her flesh, how much more love and care must not one have for him who is his brother according to the Spirit? And if any of them becomes sick, the other friars are to take that care of him which they would wish to have themselves.

7. The Penance to be imposed on Friars who sin

Should any friars succumb to the temptations of the enemy and fall grievously into such sins as may have been reserved among the friars to the ministers provincial, then such friars must betake themselves to the ministers as soon as possible, without delay. If the ministers are priests, they are with mercy to impose a penance upon them. If they are not priests, they should have such a penance imposed by some priest of the Order as may seem to them most advisable according to the will of God. They must take care likewise not to be angered or disturbed because of the sin which another may commit, since anger and anxiety hinder charity in themselves and in the sinners.

8. The Election of the Minister General of this Brotherhood, and the Chapter of Pentecost

All the friars are to be bound always to have one of the friars of this religion [the Order] as Minister General and servant of the whole brotherhood, and they are to be held to strict obedience to him. In the event of his death, the choice of a successor is to be made by the ministers provincial and custodes at the Chapter of Pentecost. The ministers provincial are always bound to convene for this chapter, wherever the minister general shall have decreed; and this once every three years, or at a longer or shorter interval, as the same minister general may have decided. If it should ever become evident to the whole of the ministers provincial and custodes that the minister general is not equal to the task of serving the friars and promoting their general welfare, then these same friars must in the name of the Lord, since the election is committed to them, choose someone else as their leader. After the Chapter of Pentecost each minister and custos may, if he so wishes and it seems useful to him, call together the friars of his jurisdiction to a chapter once in the same year.

9. On Preachers

The friars are not to preach in any diocese where the bishop may have refused them permission. No friar, moreover, under any circumstances shall be so bold as to preach to the people before the Minister General of this brotherhood shall have examined and approved him and have conceded to him the office of preaching. Those thus appointed I advise and beseech that in their preaching they use words that are well-chosen and chaste, to instruct and edify the people. Let them speak to them of vices and virtues, punishment and glory, in a discourse that is brief, because it was in few words that the Lord preached while on earth.

10. How the Friars are to be Admonished and Corrected

Those friars who are the ministers and servants of the other friars should visit their friars and duly admonish and correct them in humility and charity. They shall never command them to do anything that is against their conscience and our Rule. On the other hand, the friars who are subject to them are always to bear in mind that they have given up their own will for God. For this reason I strictly command them to obey their ministers in all those things which they have promised the Lord and which are not against conscience and our Rule. And should there be friars anywhere who know and recognize that they cannot observe the Rule according to its true spirit, it is their duty and right to go to the ministers for help. On their part, the ministers are to welcome them with great love and kindness, and be so approachable toward them that these friars may speak with them and act as masters deal with servants. This is indeed as it should be, that the ministers be the servants of all the friars.

At the same time I warn the friars and implore them in the Lord Jesus Christ, that they keep themselves from all pride, vainglory, envy, avarice, the cares and worries of this world, detraction and complaint. And those who have no book-learning should not set their heart on acquiring it. Instead, let them pursue what above all else they must desire: to have the spirit of the Lord and the workings of His grace, to pray always to Him with a clean heart, and to have humility, patience in persecution and weakness, and to love those who persecute us or rebuke us; for the Lord says: "Love your enemies, and pray for those who persecute and calumniate you" (Mt. 5, 44). "Blessed are they who suffer persecution for justice' sake: for theirs is the kingdom of heaven" (Mt 5, 10). "He that shall persevere unto the end, he shall be saved" (Mt. 10, 22; Vulgate).

11. That the Friars are not to enter the Monasteries of Nuns

I strictly command all the friars not to have any associations or meetings with women which could arouse suspicion. Moreover, with the exception of those granted special permission by the Apostolic See, they are not to enter the monasteries of nuns. Again, to avoid what might provoke scandal either among the friars or about them, they are not to act as godfathers for men or women.

12. Of those who go among the Saracens
and others not of the Faith

Those friars who under divine inspiration may wish to go among the Saracens and other unbelievers are to ask leave therefor from the ministers provincial. The ministers in turn are to grant permission only to those whom they judge capable of such a vocation.

In addition, I charge the ministers by obedience to ask of the Lord Pope one of the cardinals of the Holy Roman Church, to be ruler, protector and corrector of this brotherhood, to this end: that always submissive to the same Holy Church, prostrate at her feet, and firm in the Catholic faith, we may observe the poverty and humility and the Holy Gospel of our Lord Jesus Christ, as we have firmly promised.

POVERTÀ
FRATERNITÀ
CARITÀ
...DIENZA
PRE
GHIERA
DEVOZION
ALLA
CHIESA

THE RULE FOR HERMITAGES

Francis and his followers, as we well know, went among the people, preaching, exhorting, reconciling, bringing men back to God. But we must not overlook what was likewise an essential part of their vocation: to seek God in quiet and contemplation, often for periods of time in hermitages hidden in the hills or solitary places along rivers or buried in the woods. As a result Francis wrote a Rule for such places and for the friars who dwelt in them, with emphasis on their life of prayer.

THE RULE
FOR HERMITAGES

1 Those who wish to live the gospel life in hermitages are to be three brothers or four at most. Two of them are to be the "mothers" and have two "sons" or one at least.

2 Those who are mothers are to lead the life of Martha, and the two sons are to follow the life of Mary (Lk 10, 38-42) and are to have an enclosure in which each one shall have his cell in which he is to pray and sleep.

3 And let them always say Compline of the day immediately after sunset, and take care to maintain silence and say their Hours and rise at Matins and *seek first the Kingdom of God and His justice* (Mt 6, 33).

4 And they are to say Prime at the proper hour, and after Tierce they may break silence, and can speak and go to their "Mothers".

5 And when it may please them, they can beg an alms of them for the love of the Lord God, like little poor people.

6 And afterwards they are to say Sext and Nones; and then say Vespers at the proper hour.

7 And they are not to allow any person to enter and eat in the enclosure where they live.

8 Those friars who are the "mothers" are to take care to keep apart from any outsiders; and in obedience to their minister are to guard their "sons" from every outside contact, so that no one can speak with them.

9 And the "sons" are not to speak with any person save with their "mothers" and with their Minister or custos [regional superior] when it shall please them to visit the "sons" with the blessing of the Lord.

10 From time to time the "sons" are to assume the role of "mothers", taking turns as they have mutually decided. In this, let them faithfully and carefully observe all that is laid down above.

THE ADMONITIONS OF SAINT FRANCIS

Under this title a precious series of spiritual counsels touching primarily the life and outlook of the friars has come down to us through seven centuries. In many ways the Admonitions are among the most important of the "writings" of Saint Francis, since each is a precious pearl of spiritual wisdom. Each in some way embodies the very essence of that poverty of spirit and deep sense of brotherhood which are basic to the Franciscan observance of the Gospel.

THE ADMONITIONS OF SAINT FRANCIS

1. On the Body of the Lord

1 The Lord Jesus says to His disciples: *I am the Way, the Truth and the Life; no one comes to the Father but through Me.*

2 *If you had known Me, you would have known My Father also; and from now on you shall know Him, and you have seen Him.*

3 *Philip says to Him: Lord, show us the Father, and it is enough for us.*

4 *Jesus says to him: Am I with you so long a time, and still you do not know Me? Philip, he who sees Me sees My Father also* (Jo 14, 6-9).

5 *The Father dwells in unapproachable light* (I Tim 6, 16), and *God is spirit* (Jo 4, 24), and *no one has ever seen God* (Jo 1, 18).

6 Hence only in spirit can He be seen, for it is *the spirit that gives life; the flesh has nothing to offer* (Jo 6, 64).

7 Yet neither is the Son, inasmuch as He is equal to the Father, seen by any one other than by the Father, other than by the Holy Spirit.

8 Wherefore, all those who saw the Lord Jesus according to [His] humanity and did not see and believe according to the spirit and the divinity that He is the true Son of God, were condemned.

9 So also now all those who behold the Sacrament which is sanctified by the words of the Lord upon the altar at the hand of the priest in the form of bread and wine, and do not see and believe according to the spirit and divinity that It is truly the most holy Body and Blood of our Lord Jesus Christ, are condemned.

10 This the Most High Himself attests, who says: *This is My Body and the Blood of My New Testament [which will be poured forth on behalf of many]* (Mk 14, 22, 24);

11 and: *Who feeds on My Flesh and drinks My Blood will have everlasting life* (Jo 6, 55).

12 Wherefore the Spirit of the Lord, who dwells in His faithful ones, He it is who receives the most holy Body and Blood of the Lord.

13 All others who do not share of that Spirit and presume to receive Him eat and drink judgment to themselves (cf. I Cor 11, 29).

14 Wherefore, *O you sons of men, how long will you be dull of heart?* (Ps 4, 3).

15 Why do you not recognize the truth and believe in the Son of God? (cf. Jo 9, 35)

16 Behold: daily He humbles Himself (cf. Phil 2, 8) as when *from heaven's royal throne* (Wisd 18, 15) He came down into the womb of the Virgin.

17 Daily He Himself comes to us with like humility;

18 daily He descends from the bosom of the Father upon the altar in the hands of the priest.

19 And as He [appeared] to the Apostles in true flesh, so now also He shows Himself to us in the sacred Bread.

20 And as they by their bodily sight saw only His flesh, yet contemplating Him with the eyes of the Spirit believed Him to be very God,

21 so we also, as we see with our bodily eyes the bread and wine, are to see and firmly believe that it is His most holy Body and Blood living and true.

22 And in this way the Lord is always with His faithful, as He Himself says: *Behold I am with you until the end of the world* (Mt 28, 20).

2. On the Evil of Self-will

1 The Lord said to Adam: *Eat of any tree. But you are not to eat of the tree of knowledge of good and bad* (cf. Gen 2, 16-17).

2 He could have eaten of every tree of paradise because as long as he did not go against obedience, he did not sin.
3 For he eats of the tree of the knowledge of good who appropriates to himself his own will and prides himself on the good things which the Lord says and works in him;
4 and thus, through the suggestion of the devil and the transgression of the commandment, the fruit becomes [for him] knowledge of what is evil.
5 For that reason he must suffer punishment.

3. On Perfect Obedience

1 The Lord says in the Gospel: *He who does not renounce all that he possesses cannot be My disciple* (Lk 14, 33);
2 and again: *Whoever would save his life will lose it* (Lk 9, 24).
3 That man leaves all he possesses and loses his body who gives his whole self over to obedience in the hands of his prelate [= superior, a word St Francis never uses].
4 And whatever he does and says, provided he knows that it is not contrary to the will of the prelate and that what he does is good, that is true obedience.
5 And if at times the subject should see things which would be better and more useful for his soul than those which his prelate commands him, let him willingly sacrifice his [plans] and earnestly strive to fulfill what the prelate has decided.
6 For this is obedience that makes for charity because it is pleasing to God and to neighbor.
7 If however the superior should command something that goes against his soul, though he does not obey, let him not abandon him.
8 And if in consequence he should have suffered persecution from some, let him love them the more for God's sake.
9 For he who would rather suffer persecution than wish to be separated from his brothers, truly abides in perfect

obedience because he lays down his life for his brothers (cf. Jo 15, 13).

10 For there are many religious who, under pretext of seeing better things than those their prelates command, look back (cf. Lk 9, 62) and return to the vomit of self-will (Cf. Prov 26, 11; II Peter 2, 22).

11 Such men are murderers [spiritually] and by reason of their bad example cause many souls to be lost.

4. That No One is to take to Himself the Role of Leader

1 *I did not come to be served by others, but to serve*, says the Lord (Mt 20, 28).

2 Those who are set over others should glory only as much in this preferment as they would if they were deputed to the office of washing the feet of the brothers.

3 And if they are more upset when superiorship is taken away than they would be at the loss of the office of washing feet, so much the more do they lay up treasures for themselves to the peril of their soul.

5. That No One should be proud, but should glory in the Lord

1 Consider, O man, how great is the excellence in which the Lord God has placed you by the fact that He created and formed you to the image of His beloved Son according to the body and to [His] image according to the spirit [the inner man].

2 And all creatures that are under heaven, each in its own way, serve, know and obey their Creator better than you do.

3 And even the demons did not crucify Him, but you together with them have crucified Him and still crucify Him by taking delight in vices and sins.

4 For what reason then can you glory?

5 For if you were so clever and wise that you possessed all knowledge and knew how to interpret all kinds of language and were able to investigate in detail all the things in the heavens, in none of these things can you glory!

6 One demon in fact has known more about heavenly bodies and still knows more about things on earth than all men together, though there may have been of course some human who received from the Lord a special knowledge of the depths of wisdom.

7 In like manner, if you were more handsome and richer than all others, and even if you could work wonders, such as putting demons to flight, all these things are hurtful to you, and none really belongs to you, and you cannot glory in any of them.

8 But in this we can glory: in our infirmities, and in carrying daily the holy Cross of Our Lord Jesus Christ.

6. On the Imitation of the Lord

1 All my Brothers, let us reflect on the Good Shepherd who to save His sheep bore the sufferings of the Cross.

2 The sheep of the Lord have followed Him in tribulation and persecution, in shame and hunger, in infirmity and trial, and in many other ways; and for all this they have received everlasting life from the Lord.

3 What a great shame it is for us then, that the Saints have done great deeds and we wish to receive glory and honor simply by narrating what they did.

7. That good Works should accompany Knowledge

1 The Apostle says: *The letter kills, but the Spirit gives life* (II Cor 3, 6).

2 Those are killed by the letter who seek to know only the words themselves [of the Scriptures] that they may be regarded as more learned than others and be able to acquire great riches to leave to their kinsmen and friends.

3 And those religious are killed by the letter who do not want to follow the spirit of the word of God [the scriptures], but seek rather to know the words only and to interpret them to others.

4 And those are given [new] life by the spirit of God's words who do not attribute to themselves what learning they have or seek to have, but by word and example give credit to the Lord God Almighty, to whom belongs everything that is good.

8. That We must Avoid the Sin of Envy

1 The Apostle says: *No one can say: Jesus is Lord, save in the Holy Spirit* (I Cor 12, 3).

2 Again: *Not one of them acts rightly, no, not one* (Rom 3, 12).

3 Hence, whoever envies his brother by reason of the good that the Lord says and does in him, comes close to blasphemy, for he is envious of the Most High Himself, Who says and accomplishes all that is good.

9. On [True] Love

1 The Lord says: *Love your enemies, [do good to those who hate you, and pray for those who persecute and calumniate you]* (Lk 6, 27-28).

2 For he truly loves his enemy who does not grieve over the wrong which the other does to him,

3 but for love of God is disturbed because of the sin on the other's soul. 4 And let him show love to the other by what he does.

10. On Mortifying the Body

1 There are many who when they commit sin or suffer some wrong often blame their enemy or neighbor.

2 But this is not right, for each one has the enemy in his power, namely the body by which he sins.

3 *Blessed is that servant* then (Mt 24, 46) who ever holds
   captive such an enemy given into his power and wisely
   guards himself from it;

4 because as long as he does this, no other enemy visible
   or invisible will be able to do him harm.

11. That no one should be corrupted
by the evil of someone else

1 To the servant of God nothing should be displeasing
   save sin.

2 And in whatever way some person may sin, if the servant of God were thereby troubled or angered, save out
   of charity, he stores up guilt to himself.

3 That servant of God who does not get angry or trouble
   himself about anyone, lives uprightly and without any
   self-interest.

4 And blessed is he who does not keep back anything for
   himself, but renders *to Caesar the things that are
   Caesar's, and to God the things that are God's* (Mt 22,
   21).

12. On Knowing the Spirit of the Lord

1 Thus can the servant of God be known to share the
   Spirit of the Lord:

2 if, when the Lord should work some good through him,
   his flesh [= self-centeredness] would not thereby be
   lifted on high, because it is always contrary to anything
   good,

3 but if rather in his own eyes he were to regard himself
   as of less value and esteem himself as less than all other
   men.

13. On Patience

1 *Blessed are the peacemakers, for they shall be called
   sons of God* (Mt 5, 9). The servant of God cannot know

how much patience and humility he may have within him as long as all goes well with him.

2 But should a time come when those who should render him his due go completely against him, as much patience and humility as he then shows, so much he has and no more.

14. On Poverty of Spirit

1 *Blessed are the poor in spirit: the kingdom of God is theirs* (Mt 5, 3).

2 There are many who apply themselves to prayers and Offices, and engage in much abstinence and bodily mortification,

3 yet for a single word that seems to be an affront to their person, or for any other thing they might be deprived of, they are forthwith shocked and deeply upset.

4 Such are not poor in spirit: for he who is truly poor in spirit hates himself (Lk 14, 26) and loves those who strike him on the cheek (cf. Mt 5, 39).

15. On Peace

1 *Blessed are the peacemakers, for they shall be called the children of God* (Mt 5, 9).

2 Those are truly peacemakers who, no matter what they suffer in this world, maintain peace in soul and body [= inwardly and outwardly] for the love of Our Lord Jesus Christ.

16. On Cleanness of Heart

1 *Blessed are the pure of heart, for they shall see God* (Mt 5, 8).

2 Those are truly clean of heart who despise the things of earth, [and] seek the things of heaven, and never cease always to adore and behold the Lord God living and true with pure heart and mind.

17. On the Humble Servant of God

1 Blessed is that servant who is no more puffed up because of the good which the Lord says and works through him than for what He says and does through others.

2 That man sins who wishes to receive from his neighbor more than he is willing to give of himself to the Lord.

18. On Compassion for our Neighbor

1 Blessed is the man who bears with his neighbor in his frailties as he would wish to be helped by him if he were in a like situation.

2 Blessed is the servant who attributes all good things to the Lord God, for he who would hold back anything for himself, hides within himself the money of the Lord his God [see Mt 25, 18, on the servant who buried the money of his master], and what he thought he had shall be taken away from him (Lk 8, 18).

19. On the Humble Servant of God

1 Blessed is the servant who does not regard himself as better when he is esteemed and extolled by men than when he is considered lowly, simple and despised:

2 for what a man is before God, that he is and nothing more.

3 Woe to that religious who was placed on high by others and who of his own volition is not willing to come down.

4 And blessed is that servant who is not put in a high position of his own will and ever desires to be beneath the feet of others.

20. On the Good and the Vain Religious

1 Blessed is the Religious who has no joy or delight save in the most holy words and works of the Lord,

2   and by such means leads men to the love of God.

3   Woe to that Religious who takes delight in idle and vain words and thereby provokes men to laughter. [See the work known as *The Mirror of Perfection*, c. 96, nn. 11-12].

21. On the Frivolous and Talkative Religious

1   Blessed is that servant who when he speaks does not manifest all his affairs and thoughts under hope of some reward, and is not quick to speak (Prov 29, 20), but wisely foresees what he is to say and answer.

2   Woe to the religious who does not retain in his heart the good things the Lord has shown him and does not show them to others by his deeds, but rather in the prospect of some reward seeks to make them known to men by talking about them.

3   He is already repaid (cf. Mt 6, 2 and 16), and his hearers take away little fruit.

22. On Correction

1   Blessed is the servant who would bear discipline, accusation and reproof from another as patiently as he would from himself.

2   Blessed is the servant who, when reproved, gently submits, respectfully obeys, humbly confesses, and willingly makes satisfaction.

3   Blessed is the servant who is not quick to excuse himself and who humbly bears shame and reproach for a sin where he did not commit any fault.

23. On Humility [in a superior]

1   Blessed is the servant who is found as humble among his subjects as he would be amidst his masters.

2   Blessed is the servant who ever remains under the rod of correction.

3   He is the *faithful and wise servant* (cf Mt 24, 45), who in all his offences does not delay to punish himself, inwardly by contrition, and outwardly acknowledging his fault and making due satisfaction.

24. On True Love

Blessed is the servant who would love his brother as much when he is sick and cannot be of assistance to him as he would when he is well and can be of help to him.

25. Again on True Love

Blessed is the servant who would love and respect his brother when he is far from him as he would were he with him, and who would not say anything behind his back that he could not with charity say in his presence.

26. That the Servants of God are to honor Clerics

1   Blessed is the servant who has faith in the clerics [priests] who live upright lives according to the pattern of the Roman Church.

2   And woe to those who despise them. For even though they may be sinners, nonetheless no one is to judge them, because the Lord Himself alone reserves to Himself the right to judge them.

3   For as the ministry with which they are charged, namely of the most holy Body and Blood of our Lord Jesus Christ, which they receive and which they alone minister to others, is greater,

4   so likewise the sin of those who offend against them is greater than any sin against all other persons in this world.

27. How the Virtues drive out the Vices

1 Where there is charity and wisdom, there is neither fear nor ignorance.
2 Where there is patience and humility, there is neither anger nor worry.
3 Where there is poverty with joy, there is neither cupidity nor avarice.
4 Where there is quiet and meditation, there is neither preoccupation nor dissipation.
5 Where there is fear of the Lord to guard the door, there the enemy cannot find a way to enter (cf Lk 11, 21).
6 Where there is mercy and discretion, there is neither superfluity nor hard-heartedness.

28. On hiding the Good lest it be lost

1 Blessed is the servant who lays up a treasure in heaven (cf Mt 6, 20) of the good things which the Lord shows him, and who does not seek to manifest them to men under pretext of gain,
2 because the Most High Himself will manifest that man's works to whomsoever He may please.
3 Blessed is the servant who guards the secrets of the Lord in his heart.

A LETTER ADDRESSED TO THE WHOLE ORDER

There are many features in this Letter which reveal, or at least hint, that it was written in 1221, before or during a General Chapter or Assembly of the Order. Not least is the fact that Brother Elias [Helias] is addressed as the Minister General (in n. 2 as Friar A, an error likely for H, as in n. 38): he was indeed the Vicar of Saint Francis in the years 1221-1227. The Chronicle of Fra Jordan of Giano plainly says that on his return from the Near East Saint Francis, despite his poor health, called a Chapter of the Friars at which Elias acted as his spokesman (cf. XIII Century Chronicles, transl. by P. Hermann, Chicago 1961, 24-33). Inasmuch moreover as Friar Cesar of Speyer was to have a prominent role in the composition of the Rule of 1221 (see the note to this Rule), it seems highly probable (judging only from the frequent and apt use of Scripture) that he was of great help in drawing up this letter.

A LETTER
ADDRESSED TO
THE WHOLE ORDER

1   In the Name of the Highest Trinity and Holy Unity of the Father and of the Son and of the Holy Spirit. Amen.

2   To all the reverend and much beloved brothers, to Friar A., minister general of the religion [Order] of the Friars Minor, his lord, and to ministers [provincial] and custodes and humble priests of the same brotherhood in Christ, and to all the simple and obedient friars, from first to last,

3   brother Francis, a man of small account and much weakness, your little servant, wishes you well in Him who redeemed us and washed us clean in His most precious Blood,

4   Whom, when you hear His Name, you must adore with fear and reverence, prostrate on the ground. His Name is the Lord Jesus Christ, Son of the Most High (cf Lk 1, 32), *who is blessed forever* (Rom 1, 25).

5   Hear, my lords, sons and brothers, *and with your ears receive my words* (Acts 2, 14).

6   *Bend the ear* (Is 55, 3) of your heart and obey the voice of the Son of God.

7   Guard His precepts in the depths of your heart and fulfill His counsels with a perfect mind.

8   *Praise Him because He is good* (Ps 135, 1) and *extoll Him in your works* (Tob 13, 6),

9   because for this has He sent you unto the whole world that by word and work you may give witness to His voice and bring all to *know that there is no other almighty [God] besides Him* (Tob 13, 4).

10   *Persevere in discipline* (Hbr 12, 7) and in holy obe-

dience, and fulfill with good and firm resolve what you have promised Him.

11 The Lord God offers Himself to us as to [His] sons (cf. Hbr 12, 7).

12 To this end I beseech you, all my brothers, kissing your feet and with all the love of which I am capable, that you show all reverence and all honor, as far as in you lies, to the most holy Body and Blood of our Lord Jesus Christ,

13 in Whom the things that are in heaven and the things that are on earth are made peaceful and reconciled to Almighty God.

14 I also beseech in the Lord all my brothers who are and who will be and who hope to be priests of the Most High that whenever they wish to celebrate Mass, pure in person and pure in action, they reverently offer the true sacrifice of the most holy Body and Blood of our Lord Jesus Christ with a holy and pure intention, not for any earthly thing nor out of fear or love of any man, as though pleasing men (cf Eph 6, 6; Col 3, 22).

15 But let all their will, with the help of grace, be directed to God, in the desire to please thereby only the most High Lord Himself because He alone works therein as it pleases Him.

16 Since He Himself says: *Do this in memory of Me* (Lk 22, 19; I Cor 11, 24), if anyone should do otherwise, he becomes Judas the traitor and is guilty of the Body and the Blood of the Lord.

17 Recall to mind, my brothers who are priests, what is written in the law of Moses, that anyone transgressing even materially died *without any mercy* (Hbr 10, 28) according to the decree of the Lord.

18 *How much* greater and *worse punishments* does he not merit to suffer *who has trodden under foot the Son of God and has esteemed the blood of the testament unclean, by which he was sanctified, and has offered an affront to the Spirit of grace?* (Hbr 10, 29).

19 For a man despises, defiles and treads under foot the Lamb of God when, as the Apostle says, not recogniz-

ing and *discerning* (I Cor 11, 29) the Holy Bread of Christ from other nourishment or works, he either eats unworthily or even, if he were worthy, eats for show and so eats unworthily, since the Lord says through the prophet: *Cursed be he who does the work of the Lord deceitfully* (Jer 48, 10).

20 And the priests who will not take this to heart He in truth condemns, saying: *I will curse your blessings* (Mal 2, 2).

21 Listen, my Brothers: If the Blessed Virgin is so honored, as is meet, because she carried Him in her most holy womb; if the blessed Baptist trembled and did not dare to touch the holy head of God; if the sepulcher in which He lay for some time is held in veneration,

22 how holy, upright, and worthy must he be who holds in his hands, receives with his heart as well as by mouth, and gives to others to receive, not One who is about to die, but Him who is to conquer and is glorified forever, *on whom the angels desire to look* (I Pet 1, 12).

23 See your dignity, my brothers who are priests, and be holy, for He is holy!

24 And as the Lord God has honored you above all other men because of this ministry, so also must you more than all others love, revere and honor Him!

25 What great misery and deplorable weakness that when you can have Him thus present, you are more concerned about anything else in the whole world!

26 Let the whole man be seized with fear, let the whole world tremble, and heaven rejoice, when *Christ, the Son of the living God* (Jo 11, 27), is upon the altar in the hand of the priest.

27 O most wondrous height and stupendous honor! O sublime humility! O humble sublimity! that the Lord of the universe, God and Son of God, thus humbles Himself that for our salvation He hides Himself under an ordinary morsel of bread!

28 Behold, my brothers, the humility of God and *pour out your hearts before Him* (Ps 61, 9). Humble yourselves

that you may be exalted by Him (cf. I Pet 5, 6: Jas 4, 10).

29 Hold back nothing therefore of yourselves for yourselves, that He may receive you wholly Who gives Himself entirely to you!

30 I admonish you therefore and exhort in the Lord that in the places where the friars stay only one Mass be celebrated each day according to the form of Holy Church.

31 If there should be several priests in the place, for love of charity let one be content to hear the celebration of the other priest,

32 for the Lord Jesus Christ fills both those present and those absent who are worthy of Him.

33 Though He may seem to be in many places, He nevertheless remains undivided and knows no lessening; but One, He works everywhere as it pleases Him, with the Lord God the Father and the Holy Spirit the Paraclete, from age to age forever.

34 And, because *he who is of God hears the words of God* (Jo 8, 47), we who have been more especially deputed to the divine offices must not only hear and do what God says, but also, to impress on ourselves the greatness of our Creator and our total subjection to Him, we must take utmost care of the sacred vessels and the liturgical books which contain His holy words.

35 For this reason I admonish all my friars and encourage them in Christ, that wherever they may find the written words of God, they give them all possible reverence; and if such books are not fittingly stored or are piled together in some unseemly place,

36 they should, insofar as it concerns them, gather them up and arrange them in a becoming manner, and so honor the Lord in the words which He has spoken (cf 3 Kings, 2, 4).

37 For many things are made holy by the words of God (cf I Tim 4, 5), and in virtue of the words of Christ the Sacrament of the altar is celebrated.

38 Moreover, I confess all my sins to the Lord God,

Father, Son, and Holy Spirit, to the Blessed Mary ever Virgin, and to all the holy ones in heaven; and on earth, to Brother H. [Helias], minister of our Order, as to my lord worthy of veneration, and to the priests of our Order and to all my other blessed friars.

39 In many things I have offended by my most grievous fault, especially that I have not kept the Rule which I promised the Lord, nor have I said the Office as the Rule prescribes, either out of negligence or by reason of my infirmity or because I am ignorant and unlettered.

40 And so, because of all this, as far as I am able, I beseech my lord Brother H., the Minister General, that he cause the Rule to be observed inviolably by all;

41 and that the clerics [of the Order] say the Office with devotion before God, not attending to melody of voice but to harmony of mind, so that the voice be in tune with the inner man and the mind be in harmony with God,

42 that they may appease God by their purity of heart and not tickle the ears of the people by softness of voice.

43 For my part, I promise to hold fast to all these things as the Lord shall give me grace; and I will pass them on to the brothers who are with me, to be followed in the Office and in other prescriptions of the Rule.

44 All those friars, however, who may not wish to observe these things, I do not regard as Catholics or as my Brothers. Moreover, I do not wish to see them or talk to them until they have done penance.

45 I say the same for all others who, abandoning the discipline of the Rule, go wandering about;

46 for our Lord Jesus Christ gave His life lest He cease to be obedient to the Father most holy.

47 I, Brother Francis, unprofitable man and unworthy creature of the Lord God, say through Our Lord Jesus Christ to Brother H. [Helias], Minister General of our whole Order, and to all the other Ministers General who shall come after him and to the other custodes and guardians of the friars, who are and will be, that they have

this script with them, put it into action, and carefully preserve it.

48 And I beseech them to keep what things are written herein and see to it with all diligence that they are observed according to the good pleasure of Almighty God, now and forever, as long as this world may last.

49 And those of you who will do these things, may you be blessed by the Lord, and may the Lord be with you forever. Amen.

[Concluding Prayer]

50 Almighty, eternal, just and merciful God,
   Give to us miserable creatures to do
   For Your sake alone
   What we know You wish of us,
   And always to desire what is pleasing to You,

51 That inwardly cleansed, inwardly enlightened
   and inflamed by the fire of the Holy Spirit,
   we may follow the footsteps of Your beloved Son,
   Our Lord Jesus Christ,

52 and by Your grace alone
   come to You, O Most High,
   Who in perfect Trinity and simple Unity
   live and reign and are glorified,
   God Almighty, through all ages!
   Amen!

REGOLA + NEL NOME DEL SIGNORE INCOMINCIA LA

FORMA DI VITA DELLE SORELLE POVERE

TAMENTO NEL NOME DEL SIGNORE AMEN

LETTERE

LETTERS TO THE CUSTODES

The two Letters to the Custodes (local or regional superiors) form part of the crusade of Saint Francis for clean churches and altar-linens and fitting reverence for and proper custody of the Eucharist, as called for by the Fourth Council of the Lateran and by Pope Honorius III. Passing reference to such sacred duties is made in the Letter to the Whole Order, in that to the Rulers of the People, and in the Testament of Saint Francis. It is not without meaning for us today.

A FIRST LETTER
TO THE CUSTODES

1   To all the Custodes of the Lesser Brothers [Friars Minor] to whom this letter shall come, Brother Francis, your servant and little one in the Lord God, sends greetings with new signs of heaven and of earth which on the part of God are great and most excellent, and which by many religious and other people are considered the least of all.

2   I entreat you more than for my own sake, that when it is becoming and you see it to be necessary, you humbly beseech the clergy to venerate above all else the most holy Body and Blood of our Lord Jesus Christ and His holy written words which sanctify [consecrate] His Body.

3   They must moreover esteem as precious the chalices, corporals, ornaments of the altar, and all things that pertain to the Sacrifice.

4   And if in any place the most holy Body of the Lord be shabbily lodged, It should, according to the command of the Church, be placed by them and locked in a precious locale, and be carried [to the sick] with great veneration, and be administered to others with discretion.

5   The written words of the Lord [the missal and lectionary], wherever they may be found in dusty [and dirty] places, should be taken and stored in a proper place.

6   And in all the preaching you do, admonish the people of the need to do penance, and tell them that no one can be saved except the one who receives the most holy Body and Blood of the Lord.

7   And when It is being offered in sacrifice by the priest

upon the altar or is being carried to any place, let all the people on bended knees render praise, glory and honor to the Lord God living and true.

8 And you are so to announce and preach His praise to all the peoples, that at each hour and when the bells are rung praise and thanks always be given to Almighty God by all the people throughout the whole earth.

9 And all my brothers who are custodes, if they receive this letter and have it copied and shall keep it with them and have [more] copies made for the friars who have the office of preaching and the care of the brothers, and if they have preached to the end all that is contained in this script: let them know that they have the blessing of the Lord God and mine. And all these things should be for them a true and holy obedience. Amen.

A SECOND LETTER TO THE CUSTODES

1 To all the Custodes of the Lesser Brothers to whom this letter may come, Brother Francis, the least of the servants of God: health and holy peace in the Lord.

2 Know that in the sight of God there are some things most high and sublime which are sometimes regarded by men as lowly and of little worth;

3 and that there are other things which are grand and glittering among men which before God are counted as wholly worthless and vile.

4 I beseech you before the Lord our God as much as I can, that you give the letters which touch on the most holy Body and Blood of our Lord to the bishops and the other clerics; and that you keep in mind what we commended to you in this regard.

5 Of the other letter I am sending to you which you are to give to governors, consuls and rulers of the people, in which it is written that the Praises of God be announced among the peoples and through the public squares, make many copies immediately and with great diligence distribute them to those to whom they are to be given.

AN AUTOGRAPH FOR BROTHER LEO

An autograph, written by the hand of Saint Francis himself, now found in the Cathedral of Spoleto. The original Latin would show Francis was not too versed in the intricacies of Latin, but very conscious of the spiritual needs of Brother Leo, a priest of Viterbo (it would seem) who entered the Order as one of the early companions and became one of the secretaries of Saint Francis. A man of tender conscience, he often needed the healing graces of Saint Francis.

AN AUTOGRAPH
FOR BROTHER LEO

1 Brother Leo, wish thy Brother Francis health and peace!
2 Thus I say to thee, my son, as a mother, that all the
  words which we spoke along the road I would briefly
  sum up and counsel thee in this word; and if later thou
  shouldst wish to come to me for advice, that I counsel
  thee thus:
3 In whatever way it seems better to thee to please the
  Lord God and follow His footsteps and poverty, you [!]
  should do so with the blessing of the Lord God and my
  obedience.
4 And if it is necessary for thee for thy soul's sake or
  other consolation, thou wishest, Leo, to come to me,
  come!

A LETTER TO SAINT ANTHONY

The circumstances of this brief letter are suggested by at least one source: that though Saint Anthony came to the Friars Minor after some years as a Canon Regular in Portugal and as a man brought up in sacred theology and kindred studies, he did not wish to teach theology to the Friars, no matter how much they begged him to do so, without the express permission and consent of Saint Francis. In answer, the latter manifests his esteem of Brother Anthony (calling him "my bishop") and at the same time reveals the spirit that must guide both teacher and student. Late manuscripts change the you *to* they *to read: "they must not extinguish..." The reference to the Rule (approved by Pope Honorius III, 29 Nov. 1223) helps us to date the letter since in chapter V of the final Rule Saint Francis speaks of the manner of working: "The friars are to labor faithfully and devoutly, so that in banishing idleness, the enemy of the soul, they do not extinguish the spirit of holy prayer and devotion [total God-centerness], to which all passing things must be secondary in value" [slightly paraphrased here].*

A LETTER
TO SAINT ANTHONY

1 To Brother Anthony, my "bishop", Brother Francis
   sends greetings.
2 It pleases me that you read [= teach] sacred theology to
   the friars, provided that amid such study you do not extinguish the spirit of prayer and devotion, as is contained in the Rule.

A BLESSING FOR BROTHER BERNARD

Thomas of Celano details for us in both his biographies of Saint Francis the conversion of Bernardo di Quintavalle, an outstanding citizen of Assisi, who became the first true disciple of the Saint. He had often given him hospitality and what he saw of Francis at such close range led him to follow him (I Celano, n. 24; II Celano, n. 109). Later he went to Spain with Brother Giles, and to Bologna. Back in Assisi, he was to undergo inner trials (as St. Francis had predicted), but at the end he died in peace and joy of spirit. Little wonder that the dying Francis left him a special blessing.

A BLESSING FOR BROTHER BERNARD

1 Write as I tell you:
2 the first Brother the Lord gave me was Friar Bernard. He was the very first to begin and fulfill in a most perfect way the perfection of the Holy Gospel by distributing all his goods to the poor.
3 Because of this and many other good qualities I am bound to love him more than any Brother of the Whole Order.
4 For this reason I wish and command, as far as I can, that whoever may be the Minister General, he is to love and honor him as myself,
5 and that the ministers provincial likewise and the friars of the whole Order regard him as myself. [Cf. R.B. Brooke, *Scripta Leonis... The Writings of Leo...* 276-277].

WHAT IS PERFECT JOY

The Fioretti *(The Little Flowers of Saint Francis) are full of stories of the marvelous deeds of Saint Francis and his early companions, often in a form widely different from the original setting. One such is found in chapter 8, according to which Francis and Brother Leo are walking back from Perugia (some 20 or more kilometers away) to the Porziuncola at Assisi in cold and wintry weather. Leo precedes St. Francis by some paces (a custom the friars had at that time), while Francis probes and explains what is perfect joy. The version given here, from Brother Leonardo of Assisi, who had been the companion of Saint Francis in his journey to the East, is certainly the original form.*

WHAT IS
PERFECT JOY

1   Brother Leonard related to us that one day at Saint Mary of the Angels [the Porziuncola] the blessed Francis called Brother Leo and said: "Brother Leo, write!"

2   And he answered: "Look, I am ready!"

3   "Write", he told him, "what is true joy.

4   A messenger arrives and says that all the Masters at Paris have entered the Order. Write: this is not true joy.

5   Again: that all the prelates beyond the mountains [the Alps], archbishops and bishops; and again, that the King of France and the King of England [have entered]: write: this is not true joy.

6   Again: that my Brothers have gone to the infidels and have converted them all to the faith. Again: that I have such grace from God that I heal the sick and work many miracles: I tell you that in all these things there is not true joy!

7   But what is true joy?

8   I am returning from Perugia and in the depths of the night I come here [to the Porziuncola], and it is wintertime, muddy, and so cold that icicles form on the bottom of my tunic and hit against my legs, and blood comes out of such wounds.

9   And thus besmirched by mud and cold and ice I come to the door, and after I have knocked and called for some time, a brother comes and asks: Who's there? I answer: Brother Francis.

10   And then he says: Go away! this is not a decent hour to be going about: so you won't get in!

11   And if I would again insist, he might answer: Go away! You're no more than a simpleton and idiot, so don't

come back again! We are so numerous and such that we have no need of you!

12 And I stand again at the door and say: For the love of God take me in this night!

13 And he would respond: I will not!

14 Go to the Crosiers' place and ask them!

15 I tell you (Leo), if I would put up with all this and not be upset, in this is true joy and real virtue and the salvation of one's soul!''.

The Hospital was that of S. Salvatore delle Pareti, of the Order of the Crosiers. It was located on the road between Assisi and the Porziuncola, where the Villa Gualdi is found today. One of the Brothers there, Moricus by name, was cured by Saint Francis and subsequently joined the friars. St. Bonaventure tells of his cure, in his Legend of Saint Francis, c. 4, n. 8.

THE TESTAMENT OF SAINT FRANCIS

The circumstances which led Saint Francis to dictate this Last Will to Brother Leo, his companion and secretary (as we would say), are reflected in the so-called Testament of Siena. Six months before his death, while Francis was at Siena for treatment of his eyes, he became deathly sick (I Cel., n. 105). The friars begged him to leave some memento of his affection for them and his last will for the Order. He dictated such a document to Friar Benedict of Piratro: "Write that I bless all my Brothers who are in the Order and all those who will enter it until the end of time. Since I cannot speak because of weakness and the pains of my infirmity, briefly in these three words I make known to my Brothers what is my will; namely, as a sign that they remember my blessing and testament: that they always love one another, that they always love and respect our Lady Holy Poverty, and that they be ever faithful and subject to prelates and to all clerics of Holy Mother Church" (cf. the Legend of Perugia, n. 17, in the English Omnibus of the Sources for the Life of Saint Francis, pp. 993 f; and a protracted version in The Mirror of Perfection, c. 87, Omnibus, pp. 122 of [most probably the work of Francis Bartholi of Assisi]). Some time later Francis was able to return to Assisi, though still in poor health. Conscious that Sister Death was not far away, Francis began to compose the Testament with the aid of Brother Leo. Lodged in the Bishop's Palace (for fear that his body be stolen were he to die at the Porziuncola), he composed most if not all of the Testament ere he was brought back to Our Lady of the Angels to die. Visited by a physician from Arezzo, he was told that death would come toward the end of September or the fourth of October. Raising his arms toward heaven, he cried out with great joy: "Welcome, my Sister Death!" In a real sense, the Testament is a mirror of perfection inasmuch as not altogether inadvertently Saint Francis reveals himself as the God-given example for all who call him Father (see n. 34, below).

THE TESTAMENT OF OUR HOLY FATHER SAINT FRANCIS

1 This is how the Lord gave me, Brother Francis, the grace to begin to do penance: when I was yet in my sins, it seemed to me unbearably bitter to see lepers.

2 And the Lord himself led me among them, and I showed kindness toward them.

3 And as I went away from them, that which had seemed bitter to me was now changed for me into sweetness of mind and body. And then I tarried yet a little while, and left the world.

4 And the Lord gave me such a faith in the churches, that in a simple way I would thus pray and say:

5 "We adore You, O Lord Jesus Christ, [here] and in all Your churches which are in the whole world, and we bless You, because by Your holy Cross You have redeemed the world."

6 Then the Lord gave me, and gives me now, toward priests who live according to the norm of the Holy Roman Church, so great a confidence, by reason of their priesthood, that even if they sought to persecute me, I would nonetheless return to them.

7 And if I were to have as great a wisdom as Solomon had, and were to meet poor priests of this world, I do

not wish to preach without their consent in the parishes in which they dwell.

8 And these and all others I wish to reverence, love and honor as my lords.

9 And I do not wish to look for sin in them, because I discern the Son of God in them, and they are my lords.

10 And it is for this reason that I act thus: that in this world I see nothing with my bodily eyes of Him who is the most high Son of God except His most holy Body and most holy Blood, which they receive and which they alone minister to others.

11 And these most holy mysteries above all else I desire to be honored and adored and kept in precious places.

12 Wherever I shall find His most holy words [the reference is to Missals and Bibles] in unbecoming places, I wish to pick them up and I ask that they be removed and put in a fitting place.

13 And all theologians and those who impart the holy words of God, we must honor and reverence as those who minister to us *spirit and life* [cf. Jo 6, 64).

14 And after the Lord had given me brothers, no one showed me what I was to do, but the Most High Himself revealed to me that I should live according to the pattern of the Holy Gospel.

15 And I had it written down in few words and simple manner, and the Lord Pope [Innocent III] confirmed it to me.

16 And those who came to accept this way of life gave to the poor whatever they might have had. And they were content with one habit [cf. Mt. 10, 10; Lk 9, 3], quilted inside and out, with a cord and breeches.

17 And we had no desire for aught else.

18 The clerics among us prayed the Office like otner clerics, while the laics said the Our Father. And quite willingly we would live in [poor and abandoned] churches.

19 And we were without learning, and subject to all.

20 And I was wont to work with my hands, and I still wish to do so. And I earnestly wish that all the friars be oc-

cupied with some kind of work, as long as it becomes our calling.

21 Those who do not know how [to work] should learn, not indeed out of any desire to receive the pay which the work may bring, but to give a good example and to avoid idleness.

22 And if there are times when no pay is given for our work, let us have recourse to the table of the Lord, begging alms from door to door.

23 As our greeting, the Lord revealed to me that we are to say: "The Lord give you peace!"

24 The friars should make sure that they do not receive under any circumstances churches, houses however small and mean, and all else built for their use, unless these are truly in keeping with the holy poverty we have promised in the Rule; and, as strangers and pilgrims (I Pet 2, 11), they should always consider themselves as guests therein.

25 I firmly command all the friars by obedience that, wherever they may be, they do not dare to ask for any letter of privilege at the Roman Curia, either directly or through an intermediary, whether concerning a church or any other place, or under the pretext of preaching, or even as protection against bodily persecution.

26 Rather, if they have not been welcomed in one place, let them depart to another and there do penance with the blessing of God.

27 And it is my firm desire to obey the Minister General of this brotherhood, as likewise the guardian whom it may please him to give me.

28 And I thus wish to be a prisoner in his hands, so that I can neither move nor act apart from obedience to him and without his consent, because he is my lord.

29 And though I am simple and ailing, I wish always to have a cleric who may recite the Office with me, as it is prescribed in the Rule.

30 And all the other friars are to be bound in like manner to obey their guardians and to say the Office in the manner prescribed by the Rule.

31 And should some be found who are not saying the Office according to the prescript of the Rule but are trying to introduce some other form of it, or who are not Catholics, all the friars, wherever they are, are to be bound in obedience to present any such, wherever they may find him, to the custos nearest the place where they have found him.

32 And the custos is to be firmly bound by obedience to guard him strongly day and night like a prisoner, so that he cannot escape his hands, until he shall in his own person deliver him into the hands of his minister.

33 And the minister is to be firmly bound by obedience to send him by such friars who will day and night guard him as a prisoner until they bring him before the Lord of Ostia, who is the master of this whole brotherhood and has it under his protection and correction.

34 And the brothers are not to say: "This is another Rule", because this is a reminder of our past, an admonition and exhortation, and my Testament, which I, little Brother Francis, am making for you, my blessed Brothers, to this end, that we may observe in a more Catholic manner the Rule we have promised the Lord.

35 And the Minister General and all other ministers and custodes shall be bound by obedience not to add to these words or to take from them.

36 And let them always have this writing with them together with the Rule.

37 And in all the Chapters they hold, when they read the Rule, let them read these words also.

38 And all my Brothers, both clerics and laics, I firmly charge by obedience not to make any explanation of the Rule or of these words and say: "Thus they are to be understood."

39 Rather, as the Lord has granted me simply and plainly to speak and write the Rule and these words, so simply and without gloss you are to understand them, and carry them out by your holy deeds to the very end.

40 And everyone who shall observe these things, may he be filled in heaven with the blessing of the Most High

Father; and may he be filled on earth with the blessing
of His beloved Son in fellowship with the most Holy
Spirit the Comforter and all the powers of heaven and
all the Saints.

41   And I, Brother Francis, your little one and servant, as
much as I can, confirm to you within and without this
most holy blessing. Amen.

Part III

FRANCIS INSPIRES
THE POOR CLARES

THE PATTERN OF LIFE GIVEN SAINT CLARE

The title of this short piece derives from the Rule of Saint Clare, who tells us in chapter 6 that Saint Francis wrote a form of life for her and her Sisters. In reality, it is more of a promise than a Rule. We give the context as well as the words of Francis.

[Cf. *The Legend and Writings of Saint Clare*, translated by I. Brady. O.F.M., 1953, 73-74].

THE PATTERN OF LIFE GIVEN SAINT CLARE

1 When the Blessed Father saw that we had no fear of poverty, toil, sorrow, humiliation, or the contempt of the world, but rather that we held such things in great delight, moved by fatherly love he wrote for us a form of life as follows:

2 "Since by divine inspiration you have made yourselves daughters and handmaids of the most High and Sovereign King, the Father in Heaven, and have espoused yourselves to the Holy Spirit, choosing to live according to the perfection of the holy Gospel,

3 I will and promise on my part and that of my brothers always to have for you as for them loving care and special solicitude".

THE EXHORTATION OF SAINT FRANCIS
TO THE SISTERS AT SAN DAMIANO

The Canticle of Brother Sun is well known, as one of the greatest writings of Saint Francis. What has escaped notice until quite recently is another Song which he wrote about the same time, as he lay sick in a straw hut near San Damiano: an Exhortation to the Poor Clares to rejoice in their own vocation and sustain whatever hardships it might entail, living in harmony and love in the midst of poverty. Cf the Mirror of Perfection, *c. 90: based on the earlier work known as the* Legend of Perugia *(n. 45) or the* Compilatio Assisiensis *(ed. Assisi 1975); also found in* We Were with Saint Francis, *edited by Fr. S. Butler (Chicago 1976), 175-76. The text was known as long ago as 1941 in two manuscripts at Verona, one with the original version, another in a sixteenth-century modernization. The English rendition here is based on the earlier text.*

THE EXHORTATION OF SAINT FRANCIS TO THE SISTERS AT SAN DAMIANO

1 Listen, Little Poor Ladies called by the Lord, who have been gathered from many parts and provinces:

2 Live always in fidelity, that you may die in obedience.

3 Do not look at the life without, because that of the Spirit is better.

4 I beg you, in great love, that in using the alms the Lord gives you you provide for your needs with wise discretion.

5 Those who are afflicted with sickness, and those wearied in caring for them, should, all of you, bear it in peace.

6 For you will see how precious is such fatigue, because each of you will be crowned queen in heaven, with the Virgin Mary!

[*A later hand in both manuscripts adds a final line to the original text:* through the merits of Saint Clare. Amen]

THE LAST WILL OF SAINT FRANCIS
FOR ST. CLARE AND HER SISTERS

In Chapter VI of her Rule Saint Clare provides a second brief document from Saint Francis. "Shortly before his death," she writes, "he wrote for us his last will, saying:..." (p. 145).

[cf. *The Legend and Writings of Saint Clare*, 74. It is rather evident that this is the letter mentioned in a Perugia manuscript (n. 1046) published in several forms: the *Compilatio Assisiensis*, ed. M. Bigaroni (Latin and Italian), Assisi 1975, 40 ff; again, in *The Legend of Perugia*, n. 109, in *Omnibus of Sources*, 1084f; and *The Writings of Leo, Rufino, and Angelo*, ed. in Latin and English, ed. R.B. Brooke (Oxford 1970), n. 109, pp. 278-281.]

THE LAST WILL OF SAINT FRANCIS FOR ST. CLARE AND HER SISTERS

1 I, little Brother Francis, wish to follow the life and poverty of our Lord Jesus Christ most high and of His most holy Mother, and to persevere in this until the end.

2 And I beseech you, my Ladies, and counsel you always to live in this most holy form of life and poverty.

3 And guard yourselves well, lest by the teaching or counsel of anyone you ever in any way depart from it.

Part IV

FRANCIS TO HIS
LAY FOLLOWERS

A LETTER TO THE FAITHFUL

As Saint Francis began to send out his first Brothers to preach to the people, they sought lodging with the parish priests. When this was not possible, they would stay with layfolk who feared the Lord. Their preaching, we are told, bore much fruit: many young men joined the Friars, women soon flocked to the monasteries of the Poor Clares, married folk asked directions for a deeper Christian life. Saint Francis eagerly responded to this inner renewal of the Christian life, both by his preaching and counsel and by the Letter to the Faithful (members of such groups), found in two versions: the first, an early form, is known today only through one manuscript; the second and more definitive version, of much later date, had a very wide circulation, including at least two early translations in Italian. Such Faithful were indeed the first members of the Third Order, the Penitents, as they are called in the ancient Office for the Feast of Saint Francis.

A LETTER
TO THE FAITHFUL

1. The First Version

[AN EXHORTATION TO THE BROTHERS AND SISTERS OF PENANCE]

In The Name of the Lord
[Chapter I] On those who do penance

1 All who love the Lord with all their heart, with whole soul and mind, and with all their strength (Mk 12, 30), and love their neighbors as themselves (Mt 22, 39),

2 and hate their bodies with [their] vices and sins,

3 and receive the Body and Blood of our Lord Jesus Christ, and

4 bring forth worthy fruits of penance:

5 O how happy and blessed are men and women as long as they do such things and persevere in them,

6 because the Spirit of the Lord shall rest upon them (cf. Is 11, 2) and make His dwelling and abode in them (cf Jo 14, 23).

7 And they are children of the heavenly Father, whose works they do; and they are spouses, brothers and mothers of Our Lord Jesus Christ.

8 We are spouses when the faithful soul is joined by the Holy Spirit to our Lord Jesus Christ.

9 We are brothers to Him when we do the will of the Father who is in heaven (Mt 12, 50);

10 mothers, when we carry Him in our heart and body (cf I Cor 6,20) through divine love and a pure and sincere conscience; we bring Him to birth by our holy manner of living, which must be a shining example to others.

11 O how glorious it is, holy, and magnificent, to have a Father in heaven!

12 O how holy, consoling, beautiful and wondrous to have such a Spouse!

13 O how holy and how delightful, gratifying, [yet] humble, peaceful, sweet, lovable, and far surpassing all other desires, to have such a Brother and such a Son, our Lord Jesus Christ, who laid down [His] life for His sheep (Jo 10, 15) and prayed to the Father, saying:

14 *Holy Father, keep them in Your Name whom You have given Me in the world. They were Yours and You gave them to Me* (Jo 17, 6).

15 *And the message You entrusted to Me I have given them, and they received it, and have believed in truth that I came from You, and* have known *that it was You who sent Me* (Jo 17, 8).

16 *For these I pray, and not for the world* (Jo 17, 9).

17 *Bless and consecrate* them (Jo 17, 17). *And for their sakes I consecrate myself.*

18 *I do not pray for them alone, but also for those who will believe in Me through their word* (Jo 17, 20), *that they may be sanctified as one, as we are one* (Jo 17, 23 and 11).

19 And I wish, Father, *that where I am they also should be with Me, that they may see My glory (Jo 17, 24) in Your kingdom* (Mt 20, 21). Amen.

[Chapter II] On Those who do not do Penance

1 All those, however, both men and women, who are not living in penance and

2 who do not receive the Body and Blood of our Lord Jesus Christ

3 and are caught up in vices and sins and go the way of evil concupiscence and the evil desires of their flesh,

4 and are not faithful to what they have promised the Lord,

5 and in body are slaves to the world, the demands of the flesh and the worries of the world and the cares of this life:

6 all such are held captive by the devil, whose children

they are and whose works they do (Cf Jo 8, 41).

7 They are blind, because they do not see the true light, Our Lord Jesus Christ.

8 They lack all spiritual wisdom, because they do not possess the Son of God, who is the true Wisdom of the Father,

9 so that one can say of them: *Their wisdom has been swallowed up* (Ps 106, 27, according to the old Roman Psalter); or again: *They are accursed who turn away from Your commandments* (Ps 118, 21).

10 They see and are aware [of what they are doing]; they know, and yet do evil things, and so knowingly lose their souls.

11 O you blind ones! See how you are deceived by your enemies: by the flesh, the world, and the devil! And you do this because for fallen nature it is a delight to commit sin, and a bitter thing to make that nature serve God;

12 for all vices and sins arise in and come forth from the hearts of men, as the Lord says in the Gospel (cf Mk 7, 21).

13 And you have [gained] nothing in this world or in that which is to come.

14 Yet you imagine you will hang on to the emptiness of this world for a long time. But you are deceived! for the day and the hour will come, of which you have no knowledge or thought and which you choose to ignore. The body will sicken, death will draw near, and the man dies a bitter death.

15 And no matter where or when or how death comes, if a man dies in mortal sin without penance and satisfaction, when he can repent and does not do so, the devil snatches his soul out of his body with such anguish and distress that no one can know how to save him to whom it happens.

16 And all the riches and power and knowledge and wisdom which they thought they had will be taken from them (cf Lk 8, 18; Mk 4, 25).

17 And they leave all their substance to relatives and

friends, and these have already taken it away and divided it up, and then have said: "Cursed be his soul! He could have given us more and have accumulated more than what he really heaped up."

18 The worms feast on the body; and so such people have lost body and soul in this short life and end up in hell, where they shall be tormented without end.

19 In the love which is God (I Jo 4, 16) we beg all those to whom this letter comes, to receive with divine love and kindness these fragrant words of our Lord Jesus Christ.

20 And those who do not know how to read should have them read frequently.

21 And they should preserve them and live them in holiness unto the end, for they are *spirit and life* (Jo 6, 64).

22 And those who fail to do so will be held to render an account of them on judgment-day (cf. Mt 12, 36) before the tribunal of Our Lord Jesus Christ (cf Rom 14, 10).

2. The Later Version

In the Name of the Lord, Father and Son and Holy Spirit. Amen.

1 To all Christians, Religious, Clerics and Lay-persons, men and women, to all who dwell in the whole world, Brother Francis, their servant and subject, extends homage and reverence, true peace from heaven and sincere charity in the Lord.

2 Since I am the servant of all, I am bound to serve all and to administer the fragrant words of my Lord.

3 Hence, as I consider within me that by reason of the infirmity and weakness of my body I cannot visit each one in person, I have proposed to offer you by this present letter and message the words of Our Lord Jesus Christ, who is the Word of the Father, and the words of the Holy Spirit, which *are spirit and life* (Jo 6, 64).

4 This Word of the Father, so worthy, so holy and

glorious, the most High Father announced from heaven through His angel Saint Gabriel [to come] in the womb of the holy and glorious Virgin Mary, from whose womb He received the flesh of our humanity and weakness.

5 Who, *though He was rich* (2 Cor 8, 9) beyond all else, wished Himself together with the most blessed Virgin, His Mother, to choose poverty.

6 And when His Passion was at hand, He celebrated the Pasch with His disciples and, taking bread, gave thanks and blessed and broke it, saying: *Take and eat: this is My Body* (Mt 26, 26).

7 And, taking the chalice, He said: *This is My Blood of the New Covenant which will be poured forth for you and for many for the forgiveness of sins* (Mt 26, 28).

8 Then He prayed to the Father, saying: *Father, if it can be done, let this chalice pass from Me* (Mt 26, 39).

9 *And His sweat became like drops of blood, trickling down upon the ground* (Lc 22, 44).

10 Yet He placed His will in the will of the Father, saying: *Father, Thy will be done* (Mt 26, 42): *not as I will, but as Thou wilt* (Mt 26, 39).

11 Such was the will of the Father that His Son, blessed and glorious, whom He gave to us and who was born for us, should by His own Blood offer Himself as sacrifice and victim on the altar of the Cross,

12 not for Himself *through Whom all things were made* (cf Jo 1, 3), but for our sins,

13 leaving us an example, to follow in His footsteps (cf I Pet 2, 21).

14 Again, the Father wishes that all of us be saved through Him [the Son] and that we receive Him with our heart pure and our body chaste.

15 Yet few there are who wish to receive Him and be saved by Him, although His yoke is easy and His burden light (Mt 11, 30).

16 Those who do not wish to taste how good is the Lord (Ps 33, 9) and who love darkness rather than the light

(Jo 3, 19), not wishing to fulfill the commandments of the Lord, are cursed:

17 of them it is said by the prophet: *They are cursed who turn away from Thy commandments* (Ps 118, 21).

18 On the other hand, O how happy and blessed are those who love God and do as the Lord Himself says in the Gospel: *You shall love the Lord your God with your whole heart and with all your mind,* and *your neighbor as yourself* (Mt 22, 37 and 39).

19 Let us therefore love God and adore Him with a pure heart and pure mind, because He Himself, looking for this above all else, says: *The true adorers shall adore the Father in Spirit and in truth* (Jo 4, 23).

20 For all who adore Him must adore Him in the Spirit of truth.

21 And let us offer Him praise and prayers day and night, saying: *Our Father, who art in heaven,* because *it behooves us to pray always and not lose heart* (Lk 18, 1).

22 We must indeed confess all our sins to the priest and receive from him the Body and Blood of our Lord Jesus Christ.

23 He who does not eat His flesh and does not drink His blood *cannot enter the kingdom of God* (Jo 6, 55 and 57; 3, 5).

24 Yet let him eat and drink worthily, because he who receives unworthily *eats and drinks judgment on himself because he does not recognize the Body of the Lord* (I Cor 11, 29); that is, he does not distinguish It [from other foods].

25 Let us moreover *bring forth fruits worthy of* penace (Lk 3, 8 Vulg.).

26 And let us love our neighbors as ourselves (Mt 22, 39).

27 And if anyone does not wish to love them as himself, let him at least do no evil to them, but let him do what is good.

28 Those who have received the power of judging others should exercise judgment with mercy, as they themselves wish to obtain mercy from the Lord.

29 For, *judgment without mercy* will be theirs *who have not practiced mercy* (Jas 2, 13).

30 Let us then have charity and humility; and let us give alms, for almsgiving cleanses souls from the filth of sins (cf Tobias 12, 9).

31 For men lose all that they leave behind in this world; on the other hand, they carry with them the reward of charity and the alms they have given, for which they will receive from the Lord a reward and worthy remuneration.

32 We must also fast and abstain from vices and sins and from superfluity of food and drink, and be Catholics.

33 We must likewise visit churches frequently, and venerate and revere clerics, not so much for themselves, if they are sinners, but because of their office and administration of the most holy Body and Blood of Christ, which they sacrifice on the altar and receive and administer to others.

34 And let us all know for certain that no one can be saved except through the holy words and the Blood of our Lord Jesus Christ which clerics recite and announce and minister.

35 And they alone are to minister, and not others.

36 Yet religious, who have renounced the world, are especially bound to do more and greater things, yet not leave the ordinary things undone (cf Lk 11, 42).

37 We must hate our bodies with their vices and sins, because the Lord says in the Gospel that all evils, vices and sins come forth from the heart (Mt 15, 18-19; Mk 7, 23).

38 We must love our enemies and do good to those who hate us (see Mt 5, 44; Lk 6, 9).

39 We must keep the precepts and counsels of our Lord Jesus Christ.

40 We must also deny ourselves (Mt 16, 24) and subject our bodies to the yoke of servitude and holy obedience as each one has promised the Lord.

41 And no one is to be held by obedience to obey anyone in anything where a crime or sin is committed.

42 But let him to whom obedience is due and who is considered greater be as the lesser and the servant of the other brothers.

43 And let him have and show to each of the brothers that mercy which he would want to experience were he in a like situation (cf Mt 7, 12).

44 And let him not be angry with a brother because of his offence, but with all patience and humility let him gently admonish and encourage him.

45 We must not be wise and prudent according to worldly standards, but rather we should be truly simple, humble and empty of self.

46 And let us hold our bodies [= ourselves] in contempt because by our own fault we are all wretched and corrupt, rank and no more than worms, as the Lord says through the prophet: *I am a worm, not a man, the scorn of men, and despised by the people* (Ps 21/22 7).

47 We should never desire to be over others; but ought rather to be underlings and *subject to every human authority, for God's sake* (cf I Pet 2, 13).

48 And on all men and women, provided they have acted thus and have persevered to the end, the Spirit of the Lord shall rest (Is 11, 2) and He shall make His abode and dwelling in them.

49 And they shall be children of the heavenly Father, whose works they do.

50 And they are the spouses, brothers and sisters of our Lord Jesus Christ (cf Mt 12, 50).

51 We are spouses when by the Holy Spirit the faithful soul is joined to Jesus Christ;

52 we are His brothers when we do the will of His Father who is in heaven;

53 His mothers when we carry Him in our heart and body through love and a pure and sincere conscience; and we give birth to Him through a holy manner of living which must shine like a light as an example to others (Mt 5, 16).

54 O how glorious and holy and wondrous to have a Father in heaven!

55 O how holy, helpful, fair and wondrous to have a Spouse!

56 O how holy and beloved, well pleasing, humble, peaceful, delightful and lovable and desirable to have such a Brother and Son, who laid down His life for His sheep and prayed for us to the Father, saying: *Father, protect those in Your name whom You have given to Me* (Jo 17, 11).

57 Father, all those *whom You gave Me* in the world *were Yours and You have given them to Me* (Jo 17, 6).

58 And *the message which You gave Me, I have given to them; and they received it and have known in truth that I came from You, and have believed it was You who sent Me* (Jo 17, 8). *For these I pray and not for the world* (Jo 17, 9). *Bless and consecrate them* (Jo 17, 17).

59 *I consecrate Myself for their sakes, that they may be consecrated in one, even as We are one* (Jo 17, 19 and 11).

60 And I wish, Father, *that where I am they also may be with Me, to see My glory* (Jo 17, 24) in Your kingdom.

61 To Him who suffered so many things for us, who gave us so many blessings and will give them in time to come, let every creature that is in heaven, on earth, in the sea and in the depths, give God praise, honor, blessing;

62 for He is our strength and power, Who alone is good, alone most high, alone almighty, wondrous, glorious; and alone is holy, praiseworthy, and blessed, for ever and ever. Amen.

63 But all those who do not do penance and do not receive the Body and Blood of Our Lord Jesus Christ,.

64 who give themselves to vices and sins, and walk after evil concupiscence and evil desires, and do not keep what they have promised and

65 in body are slaves to the world, the desires of the flesh, the cares and worries of this world and the cares of this life:

66 all are deceived by the devil, whose children they are and whose works they do. They are blind because they see not the true light, our Lord Jesus Christ.

67 They do not have spiritual wisdom because they do not have the Son of God within them, who is the true wisdom of the Father. Of such it is said: *Their wisdom has been swallowed up* (Ps 106, 27).

68 They see, they recognize, they know and do evil; and wittingly lose their souls.

69 See, O you blind ones, deceived by our enemies: to wit, by the flesh, the world and the devil, see that it is pleasant to the body to commit sin and bitter to please God, because *all evils*, vices, and sins *come forth* and out of *the heart of man*, as the Lord says in the Gospel (Mk 7, 21, 23).

70 And you have nothing in this world nor in that to come.

71 You think to possess for a long while the vanities of this world, but you are deceived, for a day and an hour will come of which you think not and do not know and are ignorant of:

72 The body grows weak, death approaches, and kinsmen and friends come, saying: "Put your affairs in order".

73 And see: his wife and children, kinsmen and friends, make believe to weep.

74 And looking around, he sees them weeping, and is moved by an evil impulse; thinking within himself, he says: "Look, I place my soul and body and all my goods in your hands."

75 Verily, that man is cursed who thus entrusts and exposes his soul and body and all that he has in such hands.

76 For this reason the Lord says through the prophet: *Cursed be the man who trusts in man* (Jer 17, 5).

77 And at once they have the priest come; and the priest says: "Do you wish to receive a penance for all your sins?" He answers: "I do."

78 "Do you wish to make satisfaction, as far as you can, from your substance, for what you have done and for the things in which you have defrauded and deceived men?"

79 He answers: "No!" and the priest says: "Why not?"

80 "Because I have put everything into the hands of my relatives and friends."

81 And he begins to lose the power of speech, and thus this miserable man dies.

82 But let all know that wheresoever and howsoever a man dies in criminal sin without satisfaction when he could have made satisfaction and did not, the devil snatches his soul out of his body with such anguish and tribulation that no one can know how to save him who suffers it.

83 And all the talents and power and knowledge which he thought he possessed will be taken from him.

84 And he leaves his kinsmen and friends, and they carry off and divide his substance; and afterwards they say: "Cursed be his soul, because he could have given us more and acquired more than he did."

85 The worms eat the body; and thus he loses body and soul in this short life and will go to hell where he will be tormented without end.

86 In the Name of the Father and of the Son and of the Holy Spirit. Amen.

87 I, Brother Francis, your lesser servant, pray and beseech you in the charity which God is (cf I Jo 4, 16), and with the desire to kiss your feet, to receive, as you must, these words and others of our Lord Jesus Christ with humility and charity, and to put them into practice and observe them.

88 And all those men and women who will receive them wholeheartedly and ponder them and send copies to others, provided they shall have persevered in them to the end, may the Father and the Son and the Holy Spirit bless them. Amen!

Part V

FRANCIS
AND THE CLERGY

THE LETTER TO MEMBERS OF THE CLERGY

The great reverence Saint Francis had for the Holy Eucharist and his deep concern that friars and the secular clergy be imbued with like reverence and devotion and so be inspired thereby to proper handling and preservation of the Sacred Species, are evident in many of his writings. One such example is the present Letter to Clerics which has come down to us in an earlier version and in a revised form. These and other pieces plus some scattered references reveal what is often called the Eucharistic Crusade of Saint Francis. Undoubtedly several, if not all, are clearly inspired by the decrees (canons 19-20) of the Fourth Lateran Council, Rome 1215, and also by the Bull Sane cum olim *(22 Nov. 1219) of Pope Honorius III.*

THE LETTER
TO MEMBERS
OF THE CLERGY

1. The Early Version

1 Let all of us who are clerics ponder the great sin and ignorance which some have regarding the most holy Body and Blood of our Lord Jesus Christ and His most holy written words which consecrate the Body.

2 We know that the Body cannot be present without the words of consecration.

3 For in this world we have and see nothing in bodily form of the Most High Himself except the Body and Blood, (and) the words by which we were made and redeemed *from death to life* (I Jo 3, 14).

4 Let all those however who minister such holy mysteries ponder within themselves, especially those who minister illicitly [= against the norms of the Church], how unbecoming are the chalices, corporals and linens on which is sacrificed His Body and Blood.

5 And how It is kept by many in wretched places and carried about disrespectfully and received unworthily and indiscriminately administered to others.

6 And His written words also are sometimes trodden

under foot [the reference apparently is to a custom of storing the liturgical books on the floor near the altar]

7 And all this because *the sensual man does not perceive the things that are of God* (cf. I Cor 2, 14).

8 Does not our sense of reverence move us in respect to all such things since the good Lord Himself places Himself in our hands and we hold Him and receive Him daily in our mouth?

9 Are we unmindful that we must needs come into His hands?

10 Let us then forthwith and resolutely correct these faults and others,

11 and wherever the Most Holy Body of our Lord Jesus Christ may have been improperly reserved and abandoned, let It be removed from such a place and be put in a precious place and locked up.

12 In like manner, the written words of the Lord [the missal or the bible or lectionary] wherever they may be found in unclean places [on the dusty floor?], must be picked up and stored in a becoming place.

13 All these things, even in smaller matters, the clergy are bound above all else to carry out.

14 And those who fail to do so should be conscious that they must render an account thereof before our Lord Jesus Christ on the day of judgment.

15 That this writing may be better [known and] observed, let those who have copies made of this know that they are blessed by the Lord God.

2. The Later Version

1 Let all of us who are clerics be conscious of the great sin and ignorance which some have regarding the Most Holy Body and Blood of Our Lord Jesus Christ and His most holy written words which consecrate the Body.

2 We know that the Body cannot be present without the words of consecration.

3 For we have and see nothing in bodily form in this world of the Most High Himself except the Body and Blood, and the words by which we were made and were redeemed *from death to life* (I Jo 3, 14).

4 Let all those however who minister such most holy ministries [mysteries, in the earlier version!] consider within themselves, especially those who minister indiscreetly [illicitly, in the earler version], how unbecoming are the chalices, corporals and linens on which are sacrificed the Body and Blood of our Lord.

5 And by many It is left in wretched places, carried about disrespectfully and received unworthily and indiscriminately administered to others.

6 And His written words [missal, etc.] are also sometimes kicked around underfoot

7 because *the sensual man does not perceive the things that are of God* (cf I Cor 2, 14).

8 Does not our sense of reverence move us in respect to all such things since the good Lord Himself places Himself in our hands and we hold Him and receive Him daily by our mouth?

9 Are we not mindful that we must needs fall into His hands?

10 Let us then forthwith and resolutely correct these faults and others;

11 and wherever the Most Holy Body of Our Lord Jesus Christ may have been improperly reserved and neglected, let It be removed from such a place and be put in a precious place and locked up.

12 In like manner the written words of the Lord, wherever they may be found in dirty surroundings, must be pick-

ed up and stored in a becoming place [the reference is to missals and lectionaries].

13 And we know that we are bound above all else to observe all these things according to the precepts of the Lord and the constitutions of Holy Mother Church [the reference seems to be to the plain words of Pope Honorius III, 22 Nov. 1219, in the decree *Sane cum olim*].

14 And whoever does not do so, should know that on judgment day he is to render an account thereof before our Lord Jesus Christ.

15 That this writing may be better observed, let those who have copies made of this [for distribution] know that they are blessed by the Lord God.

Part VI

FRANCIS AND ITALY

LETTER TO THE RULERS OF THE PEOPLE

Curiously enough no manuscript-copy of this letter has come down to us, though it might likely be found in some civil archive. The text is known only through the famous Franciscan historian, Francis Gonzaga (d. 1620). Yet there can be no doubt that it is an authentic letter. Of interest is the directive or suggestion that a call to evening prayer be introduced: the fruit of St. Francis' experiences in the Near East, where he would have heard the calls to prayer from minarets. Further proof of authenticity is found in the Second Letter to the Custodes of the Order, n. 6.

LETTER
TO THE RULERS
OF THE PEOPLE

1   To all podestàs [mayors] and consuls, judges and governors, everywhere on earth, and to all others to whom this letter may come, Brother Francis, your servant in the Lord God, little and contemptible, wishes health and peace to all of you.

2   Pause and see that the day of death is nigh at hand.

3   I implore you therefore, with all the respect I can, that by reason of the cares and worries of this world which you have, you do not forget the Lord and turn away from His commandments, because all those who do forget him and turn away from His commands are accursed, and will be forgotten by Him (Ezech 33, 13).

4   And when the day of death comes, all that they thought they possessed shall be taken from them (cf Lk 8, 18).

5   And the wiser and more powerful they were in this world, so much the greater will be the torments they will endure in hell (cf Wisdom 6, 7).

6   For this reason I strongly advise You, my lords, to put aside all care and solicitude and gladly receive the most holy Body and the most holy Blood of our Lord Jesus Christ in the holy commemoration of Him [= the Mass!].

7 And You should stir up such great honor to the Lord among the people committed to You that each evening a herald should proclaim or some other sign announce that praise and thanksgiving be offered to the Lord God Almighty by all the people.

8 And if You have not done this, know that You must render an account before the Lord Your God Jesus Christ on the day of judgment.

9 Whoever will keep this writing with them and fulfill it in action, let them know that they are blessed by the Lord God.

Part VII

FRANCIS
AND ECOLOGY

SAINT FRANCIS
PATRON
OF ECOLOGISTS

To those who know Saint Francis, his life, his attitudes, his spiritual outlook, it will not have come as a surprise that at the request of the international "Planning Environmental and Ecological Institute for Quality Life" our Holy Father Pope John Paul II should have designated him (on Nov. 29 1979) as the heavenly patron of those scientists and students who are concerned with the physical wellbeing of planet Earth and indeed of the universe itself. (The Apostolic Letter is found in the Acta Apost. Sedis *71, 1979, p. 1509; and in the* Acta Ordinis Minorum *99, 1980, 24).*

No commentary accompanied or followed the brief document. Perhaps none was needed. As it stands, however, it does not forthwith make Saint Francis patron of the environment of Mother Earth or Brother Sun and Sister Moon (titles he delighted in), though some (Friars included) have so construed the document. Since then no reference to it has been made by the Pope in any public address.

But in truth, ever since Saint Francis composed his Canticle of Brother Sun (see Part I, n. 2, above), which is also called The Praises of Creatures, he has been regarded as the herald of the beauty of God's world. That world, our world, was for him as for us a place of pilgrimage. Nonetheless, he saw it likewise as the revelation of the Creator. This aspect of his spiritual vision is capsuled once for all in The First Life *of Saint Francis, which Friar Thomas of Celano composed at the bidding of Pope Gregory IX, who as Cardinal Hugolinus had been a most dear friend and adviser of the Saint ("his saint" he used to say). Two lengthy paragraphs (nn. 80-81, in Part I, Chapter 29), clearly describe "the love he had toward all creatures by reason of their Creator":*

It would take too long and be well nigh impossible to gather together and recount all that the glorious Father Francis did and taught while he lived among men. For who could ever describe his great love whereby he was caught up in all things that belong to God? Who would be able to tell of the joy he felt as he contemplated in creatures the wisdom of the Creator, His power and His goodness? In very truth a marvelous and indescribable joy would often fill him when he beheld the sun and gazed at the moon, the stars, and the whole sweep of the heavens. Oh what simple piety and pious simplicity!

Even for worms he had great affection because he had read what was said of the [suffering] Savior: "I am a worm and not a man" (Ps. 21,7). Moreover, he would pick them up along the road and put them in a safe place where they would not be trodden underfoot. What shall I say of other lowly creatures? we know that in winter, concerned about the bees lest they die of the cold, he would prepare honey and good wine for them! Their remarkable way of working stirred him to such praise of the Lord that he would often spend a whole day in such prayer, lauding them and other creatures of the Lord. Indeed, filled with the Spirit of God, he did not cease to glorify, praise and bless the Creator and Lord of all in all the elements and creatures.

The beauty of the flowers brought him great delight of soul in their shape and color and sweet odor, and thus lifted his heart and soul to Him who is the Flower of Jesse. And when he came upon a field of flowers, he would preach to them as though they understood him and would invite them to praise the Lord. He often did the same in fields of grain, in vineyards, in the woods, the while he called on all things, earth and fire, air and wind, to love the Lord and serve Him! Truly, even then he had attained the freedom of the glory of the children of God! (Rom 8, 1).

There was, no doubt, a certain ecological concern in Francis' approach to creatures. They are God's creatures, and have some kinship with us humans; otherwise he would not have called them our brothers and sisters. Yet the source of such an outlook is to be found in faith and not in fancy. If he loved all creatures, it was because he loved God so much more. If he delighted in them, respected and even venerated them, it was because they too have a God-given role to play on this planet or off in space, as do Brother Sun and Sister Moon and all the stars and planets. In consequence, in every creature he praised the Creator; in every work he glorified the Craftsman. Wisdom indeed reaches from end to end and governs all things well (Wisdom 8, 1).

What emerges from the approach of Saint Francis to creatures is his deep faith which gave him insight, the grace to see God in everyone, in everything, in all creation, in all history, and in the gift of each day, of each person he met, of each creature, rational or purely animal or material, he chanced upon. If the day was bright, blessed be the Lord! If it was murky or wet, blessed be God! If Mother Earth was covered with snow, or sloshed us with mud, blessed be God! If Brother Sun shone, God be praised! If foul weather hid the Sun, God be praised!

"ALL YOU WORKS OF THE LORD, BLESS THE LORD! AND LET US PRAISE AND EXALT HIM FOREVER!"
(Praises at Every Hour, v. 5)

Stampa
Studio VD
Città di Castello (PG)
studio.vd@virgilio.it